Ruby Essentials, A Comprehensive Guide to Becoming a Ruby Master

Learn the Core Concepts of Ruby and Build Elegant, High-Quality Code

Booker Blunt

Rafael Sanders

Miguel Farmer

Boozman Richard

Contents

How to Scan a Barcode to Get a Repository

1. **Install a QR/Barcode Scanner** – Ensure you have a barcode or QR code scanner app installed on your smartphone or use a built-in scanner in **GitHub, GitLab, or Bitbucket.**

2. **Open the Scanner** – Launch the scanner app and grant necessary camera permissions.

3. **Scan the Barcode** – Align the barcode within the scanning frame. The scanner will automatically detect and process it.

4. **Follow the Link** – The scanned result will display a **URL to the repository.** Tap the link to open it in your web browser or Git client.

5. **Clone the Repository** – Use **Git clone** with the provided URL to download the repository to your local machine.

Chapter 1: Introduction & Setup

1. Introduction

Ruby is not just another programming language—it is a philosophy. Born in the mid-1990s in Japan, Ruby was designed by Yukihiro "Matz" Matsumoto with a clear vision: to make programming not only powerful but also enjoyable. The language's elegant syntax and expressive style have earned it a dedicated following around the world, fostering a vibrant community that values both simplicity and creativity.

In today's fast-paced technological landscape, Ruby remains relevant by empowering developers to write code that is both elegant and effective. Whether you're a beginner taking your first steps into the world of programming, a seasoned professional looking to expand your toolbox, or a hobbyist eager to build something fun, Ruby offers a welcoming environment that caters to all levels of expertise. This chapter will guide you through Ruby's origins, philosophy, and community, then lead you through setting up your development environment, and finally, help you write your very first "Hello, World!" script.

Why Ruby Matters

Ruby's design centers on the belief that programming should be both enjoyable and productive. Matsumoto wanted a language that prioritizes human needs, emphasizing readability and simplicity. This focus on human-centric design means that Ruby code tends to be concise and intuitive. By reducing the cognitive load on developers, Ruby allows you to concentrate on solving problems rather than wrestling with complex syntax.

The language's philosophy—"minimizing programmer suffering"— resonates strongly with those who have experienced the frustrations of clunky code and convoluted debugging sessions. Ruby's natural syntax and built-in object-oriented features allow for rapid prototyping and quick iterations, making it an ideal tool for startups, agile teams, and individual developers alike.

A Brief History

Ruby was introduced in 1995 and quickly captured the imagination of developers worldwide. Inspired by languages such as Perl, Smalltalk, and Lisp, Matsumoto's goal was to combine the best elements of these languages while improving on their shortcomings. Ruby's unique blend of functional and object-oriented programming paradigms, along with its focus on simplicity, set it apart from its contemporaries.

Over the years, Ruby evolved from a niche scripting language into a robust tool for building scalable web applications, notably through the popular Ruby on Rails framework. Despite waves of new languages and frameworks entering the market, Ruby's emphasis on developer happiness and productivity has helped it maintain a loyal and passionate community.

Key Concepts and Terminology

Before diving deeper, it's important to familiarize yourself with some key Ruby concepts:

- **Object-Oriented:** In Ruby, everything is an object. Even simple data types like numbers and strings are objects, meaning they come with methods that can be used to perform operations on them.

- **Dynamic Typing:** Ruby is dynamically typed, which means you don't have to explicitly declare variable types. This allows for rapid development but requires careful testing.

- **Garbage Collection:** Ruby automatically manages memory, which reduces the burden on developers to manually handle resource allocation and cleanup.

- **Convention over Configuration:** Ruby, especially when used with Ruby on Rails, emphasizes sensible defaults. This principle minimizes the number of decisions developers need to make, streamlining the development process.

- **Community-Driven:** One of Ruby's greatest strengths is its community. From open-source gems (libraries) to detailed documentation and active forums, there's an abundance of resources to support your learning journey.

Setting the Tone

As you progress through this book, remember that learning Ruby is not about memorizing syntax or mastering abstract concepts—it's about embracing a mindset that values simplicity, clarity, and creativity. This chapter will lay the foundation by offering both historical context and hands-on experience with setting up your environment and writing your first script. Whether you're looking to develop web applications, automate tasks, or simply explore programming for fun, Ruby's approachable nature will empower you to tackle challenges with confidence.

2. Core Concepts and Theory

In this section, we'll dive deeper into the core concepts that define Ruby and its underlying philosophy. Understanding these concepts is critical, as they form the basis of how Ruby is structured and why it remains a favorite among developers. We will discuss Ruby's dynamic nature, object orientation, and how its flexible design encourages creativity while maintaining clarity.

The Ruby Philosophy

At the heart of Ruby lies a set of guiding principles that shape the language's design. These include:

- **Developer Happiness:** Ruby was designed with the end-user in mind—the developer. The syntax is intentionally designed to be as natural as possible, almost mimicking the flow of human language.

- **Simplicity and Elegance:** The language avoids unnecessary complexity. Its design encourages you to write clear, concise code that is both easy to read and maintain.

- **Flexibility:** Ruby's dynamic nature allows you to modify classes, add methods to existing objects, and even alter the behavior of core components. This flexibility can be a double-edged sword, but when used judiciously, it leads to incredibly expressive code.

- **Convention Over Configuration:** Borrowing this principle from Rails, Ruby's ecosystem often defaults to a "sensible default" approach. This means that many routine decisions are made for you, reducing the cognitive load and allowing you to focus on the task at hand.

Object Orientation in Ruby

One of Ruby's most powerful features is its pure object-oriented approach. Unlike languages that treat functions and procedures as separate entities, Ruby treats everything—from numbers to classes—as objects. This means that every element in Ruby has associated behaviors and properties. Let's break down what this means in practice:

- **Classes and Objects:** A class in Ruby is like a blueprint for objects. When you create an object, you are instantiating a class. For example, when you create a new string, you're actually creating an instance of the String class.

- **Methods:** Methods are functions that belong to an object. They define the behaviors that an object can perform. In Ruby, you can call methods on any object, including literals. For instance, "hello".upcase converts the string to uppercase.

- **Inheritance:** Ruby supports inheritance, allowing classes to derive behavior from other classes. This enables code reuse and the creation of complex, hierarchical structures.

- **Mixins:** Instead of multiple inheritance, Ruby offers mixins through modules. You can include modules in classes to share behavior across disparate classes without tightly coupling them.

Dynamic Typing and Flexibility

Ruby is dynamically typed, meaning you don't need to declare a variable's type explicitly. This can speed up development significantly. For example, you can write:

```ruby
```

```ruby
message = "Hello, Ruby!"
number  = 42
```

Here, Ruby automatically understands that message is a string and number is an integer. This dynamic nature is both liberating and requires careful testing, as type-related errors may only appear at runtime.

Moreover, Ruby allows for runtime modifications. You can add methods to existing classes or even change an object's state dynamically. This level of flexibility means that you can often tailor the language to fit your needs without being constrained by rigid syntax or structure.

Real-World Analogies

Imagine Ruby as a set of high-quality tools in a craftsman's toolbox. Each tool (object) is carefully designed for a specific purpose, yet all are engineered to work together harmoniously. Just as a master carpenter selects the right tool to carve intricate designs, a Ruby developer chooses the appropriate class or method to craft a solution elegantly. The language's dynamic features are like custom-made attachments that can be added on the fly, ensuring your toolkit adapts to any challenge you might face.

The Ruby Community and Ecosystem

Beyond the code itself, Ruby is renowned for its warm, welcoming community. Online forums, local meetups, and annual conferences create a vibrant network of enthusiasts who are always willing to lend a helping hand. Open-source libraries, known as gems, are a testament to this collaborative spirit—providing pre-built solutions for nearly every problem you might encounter. Whether you're debugging a tricky piece of code or looking for the latest gem, the community is an invaluable resource.

As you continue to learn Ruby, you'll find that the community not only supports you through technical challenges but also inspires creativity and innovation. From contributing to open-source projects to attending local user groups, engaging with the Ruby community can significantly enhance your skills and broaden your professional network.

3. Tools and Setup

Before you can start coding in Ruby, you need to set up your development environment. In this section, we'll go through the necessary tools, provide detailed installation instructions, and offer visual aids to guide you through the process.

Required Tools and Platforms

To follow along with this chapter and start developing Ruby applications, you'll need the following:

- **Ruby Interpreter:** The core software that will execute your Ruby code.

- **Version Manager:** Tools like RVM (Ruby Version Manager) or rbenv that help you manage multiple Ruby versions.

- **Code Editor or IDE:** An editor of your choice (e.g., Visual Studio Code, Sublime Text, Atom) that supports Ruby syntax highlighting.

- **IRB (Interactive Ruby):** A REPL (Read-Eval-Print Loop) environment that allows you to test Ruby code snippets interactively.

- **Terminal or Command Prompt:** The interface through which you will run commands, install gems, and execute Ruby scripts.

Installing Ruby Using RVM or rbenv

Using a version manager like RVM or rbenv is highly recommended. These tools let you easily switch between different Ruby versions and maintain isolated environments for your projects.

Installing RVM

1. **Install GPG Keys:**

   Open your terminal and run the following command to install the necessary **GPG** keys for verifying **RVM:**

bash

```
gpg --keyserver hkp://pool.sks-keyservers.net --recv-keys 409B6B1796C275462A1703113804BB82D39DC0E3
```

2. **Install RVM:**

   Next, install **RVM** by running:

bash

```
\curl -sSL https://get.rvm.io | bash -s stable
```

3. **Load RVM:**

   Once installed, load **RVM** into your shell session:

bash

```
source ~/.rvm/scripts/rvm
```

4. **Install Ruby:**

   Now you can install Ruby. For example, to install Ruby 3.0.0, type:

bash

```
rvm install 3.0.0
rvm use 3.0.0 --default
```

Visual Aid:

Imagine a flowchart that starts with "Download RVM" and leads through "Install RVM," "Load into Shell," and finally "Install Ruby." (See Diagram 1 below.)

Diagram 1

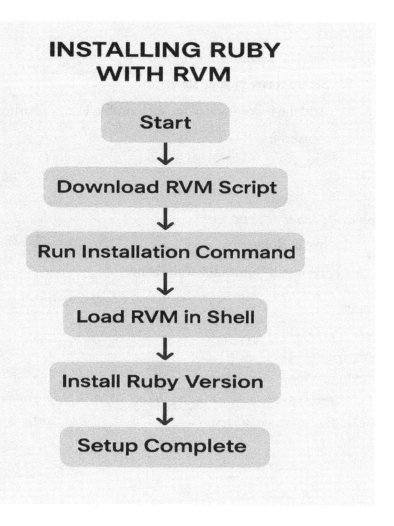

Installing rbenv

Alternatively, you can use rbenv:

1. **Install rbenv and ruby-build:**

   If you're on macOS, you can install rbenv with Homebrew:

```bash
```

```bash
brew install rbenv ruby-build
```

2. **Set up rbenv in your shell:**

   Add the following to your shell profile (e.g., ~/.bashrc or ~/.zshrc):

```bash
```

```bash
eval "$(rbenv init -)"
```

3. **Install Ruby:**

   To install Ruby 3.0.0 with rbenv:

```bash
```

```bash
rbenv install 3.0.0
rbenv global 3.0.0
A side-by-side comparison chart of RVM vs. rbenv can
help you decide which tool to use. (See Table 1
below.)
```

Table 1: RVM vs. rbenv Comparison

Feature	RVM	rbenv
Installation Ease	One-line install script	Homebrew-friendly (macOS)
Version Management	Extensive feature set	Lightweight, simpler functionality
Community Support	Large, active community	Widely used in many environments

Setting Up Your Code Editor

A modern code editor can make your Ruby development experience more enjoyable. Many editors offer Ruby plugins for syntax highlighting, code formatting, and debugging.

Visual Studio Code (VS Code)

1. **Download and Install VS Code:**

   Visit the official VS Code website and download the version for your operating system.

2. **Install Ruby Extensions:**

   Open VS Code, go to the Extensions view (Ctrl+Shift+X or Cmd+Shift+X), and search for "Ruby." Install the extension by Peng Lv or other popular Ruby extensions.

3. **Configure the Editor:**

   Adjust settings like indentation, font size, and theme to suit your preferences. You can add these settings to your VS Code settings file (settings.json):

```json
{
  "editor.tabSize": 2,
  "files.trimTrailingWhitespace": true,
  "ruby.format": "rubocop"
}
```

Other Editors

- **Sublime Text:**
  Install Package Control, then add the "Ruby" package for syntax support.

- **Atom:**
  Atom users can install language-ruby for enhanced Ruby support.

Using IRB: Your Interactive Ruby Shell

IRB (Interactive Ruby) is a powerful REPL that lets you experiment with Ruby code in real time. It's an excellent tool for testing ideas, learning the language, or debugging small pieces of code.

1. **Launching IRB:**
   Open your terminal and type:

```bash
```

```
irb
```

You will see a prompt where you can start typing Ruby commands.

2. **Simple Experimentation:**

   Try typing:

```
ruby
```

```
puts "Hello, Interactive Ruby!"
```

Notice how **IRB** immediately evaluates the command and outputs the result.

3. **Exploring Ruby Objects:**

   Since everything in Ruby is an object, you can inspect methods directly:

```
ruby
```

```
"hello".methods.sort
```

This command displays a sorted list of all methods available on a string object.

---

4. Hands-on Examples & Projects

Now that your development environment is set up, it's time to dive into hands-on coding. In this section, we'll walk you through writing your first Ruby program—a classic "Hello, World!" script—and then build on that foundation with additional examples that demonstrate core Ruby concepts.

Project 1: Your First "Hello, World!" Script

Writing "Hello, World!" is a tradition in programming—a simple program that introduces you to the basics of syntax and code execution.

Step-by-Step Walkthrough

1. **Open Your Editor:**

   Launch your preferred code editor (e.g., VS Code, Sublime Text, or Atom).

2. **Create a New File:**

   Name the file hello_world.rb.

3. **Write the Code:**

   Enter the following Ruby code:

```ruby

# hello_world.rb
# This script prints "Hello, World!" to the console.
puts "Hello, World!"
```

The puts method outputs the given string to the console.

4. **Save the File:**

   Save your file in a directory where you can easily access it from your terminal.

5. **Run the Script:**

   Open your terminal, navigate to the directory containing your file, and type:

```bash
bash
```

```
ruby hello_world.rb
```

You should see:

```
Hello, World!
```

Code Explanation:

- The # symbol is used for comments—lines that Ruby ignores during execution.

- puts is a built-in Ruby method that prints a string followed by a newline.

- The string "Hello, World!" is enclosed in double quotes.

Project 2: Building a Mini Calculator

Now, let's build a slightly more complex project—a mini calculator that performs basic arithmetic operations. This project reinforces your understanding of Ruby's syntax, user input, and control structures.

Step-by-Step Instructions

1. **Create a New File:**

   Name the file calculator.rb.

2. **Write the Code:**

   Enter the following code:

```ruby

# calculator.rb
# A simple calculator that performs basic arithmetic
operations.

def add(a, b)
  a + b
end

def subtract(a, b)
  a - b
end

def multiply(a, b)
  a * b
end

def divide(a, b)
```

```ruby
  if b == 0
    "Error: Division by zero!"
  else
    a.to_f / b
  end
end


# Greet the user
puts "Welcome to the Mini Calculator!"
puts "Enter the first number:"
num1 = gets.chomp.to_f

puts "Enter an operator (+, -, *, /):"
operator = gets.chomp

puts "Enter the second number:"
num2 = gets.chomp.to_f

result = case operator
         when '+' then add(num1, num2)
         when '-' then subtract(num1, num2)
         when '*' then multiply(num1, num2)
         when '/' then divide(num1, num2)
         else "Invalid operator!"
         end

puts "Result: #{result}"
```

3. **Understanding the Code:**

- o The script defines four methods for arithmetic operations.

- o It uses gets.chomp to capture user input from the terminal.

- o A case statement selects the appropriate operation based on the operator entered.

4. **Run the Script:**

   In your terminal, navigate to the directory containing calculator.rb and run:

```bash
```

```
ruby calculator.rb
```

5. **Try Different Operations:**

   Experiment by entering different numbers and operators. Notice how the calculator handles division by zero gracefully.

Visual Aid:

A diagram illustrating the calculator's logic flow—from input, through decision-making with the case statement, to output—can help solidify understanding. (See Diagram 2.)

Diagram 2: Calculator Logic Flow

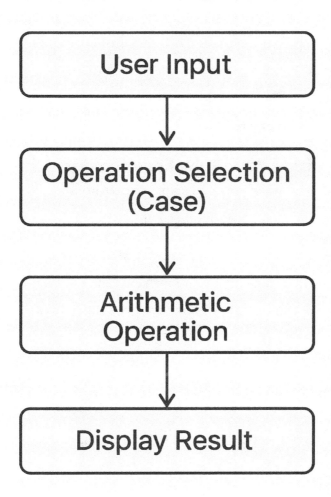

Calculator Logic Flow

5. Advanced Techniques & Optimization

While the primary goal of this chapter is to get you started, it's also important to introduce some advanced techniques and optimization strategies that even beginners can benefit from as they progress. This section will provide insights into fine-tuning your development environment and code, and it lays the groundwork for deeper exploration in later chapters.

Customizing Your Ruby Environment

Ruby's flexibility allows you to tailor your environment to suit your workflow. Here are some advanced tips:

- **Using Bundler for Dependency Management:**
  Bundler streamlines gem management, ensuring that you have consistent environments across different projects.

```bash
```

```bash
gem install bundler
bundler init
```

Edit your Gemfile to list required gems and run:

```bash
```

```bash
bundle install
```

- **Optimizing IRB:**

  Enhance your IRB session by installing the pry gem, which offers a more powerful interactive shell.

bash

```
gem install pry
```

Replace IRB with Pry by simply typing pry in your terminal.

- **Automated Code Formatting:**

  Tools like RuboCop not only check your code against style guidelines but can also auto-correct many issues.

bash

```
gem install rubocop
rubocop --auto-correct your_script.rb
```

Performance Considerations

Even in simple scripts, performance optimization is a valuable skill. Here are some techniques to consider:

- **Memory Management:**

  Ruby's garbage collector is designed to handle most tasks automatically. However, be mindful of object creation in loops. For example, avoid creating unnecessary objects inside frequently executed blocks.

- **Efficient Data Structures:**

  Choose the appropriate data structures—such as arrays, hashes, or sets—for your needs. For example, if you need fast lookup times, a hash may be more suitable than an array.

- **Profiling Your Code:**

  Use Ruby's built-in profiling tools to identify bottlenecks.

ruby

```ruby
require 'profile'
```
Insert this at the top of your script to see performance statistics.

Advanced Code Techniques

As you progress, you'll encounter scenarios that require more sophisticated techniques. Consider the following:

- **Lazy Evaluation:**

  For processing large data sets, Ruby's Enumerator class supports lazy evaluation, which can save memory and processing time.

ruby

```ruby
numbers = (1..Float::INFINITY).lazy.select { |n|
n.even? }
p numbers.first(10)
```

- **Threading and Concurrency:**

  Although this chapter focuses on basic setup, Ruby's thread

support enables concurrent programming. Experiment with threads to understand how Ruby handles parallel tasks.

A flowchart showing the decision-making process for performance optimization (e.g., "Do you have memory issues?" → "Consider lazy evaluation or a more efficient data structure") can be very useful. (See Diagram 3.)

Diagram 3: Performance Optimization Flowchart

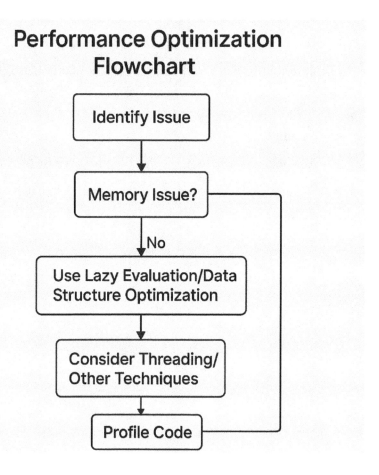

Best Practices for Production-Ready Code

While our projects in this chapter are simple, adopting best practices early on sets the stage for writing production-quality code later:

- **Consistent Code Style:**

  Follow community style guides (e.g., Ruby Style Guide) and use automated tools to enforce consistency.

- **Documentation:**

  Write clear comments and documentation. Each method should have a descriptive comment explaining its purpose and usage.

- **Testing:**

  Although not the focus of this chapter, writing tests with frameworks like RSpec or Minitest can help catch errors early.

  For example:

ruby

```ruby
# calculator_spec.rb
require_relative 'calculator'
describe "Calculator" do
  it "adds two numbers correctly" do
    expect(add(2, 3)).to eq(5)
  end
```

```
end
```

---

6. Troubleshooting and Problem-Solving

No setup process is without its challenges. In this section, we'll explore common issues that you might encounter during your Ruby journey, along with practical solutions and troubleshooting tips.

Common Installation Issues

1. **Ruby Not Found Error:**

   If you encounter an error stating that Ruby is not installed or cannot be found, ensure that your version manager (RVM or rbenv) is correctly set up in your shell profile. Verify by running:

```bash
```

```bash
ruby -v
```

If this command returns an error, double-check your installation steps and environment variables.

2. **GPG Key Verification Failures (RVM):**

   Sometimes, GPG key retrieval can fail. In such cases, try a different keyserver or use:

```bash
```

```
gpg --keyserver hkp://keys.gnupg.net --recv-keys
<KEY_ID>
```

3. **Permission Issues:**

   You might run into permissions issues when installing gems or using certain directories. Using a version manager helps isolate these issues, but you may also need to adjust file permissions or use a tool like rbenv to avoid conflicts.

Debugging Code Errors

When you run your Ruby scripts, you may encounter syntax errors or runtime exceptions. Here are some tips for debugging:

- **Read the Error Message Carefully:**

  Ruby's error messages are often descriptive. Identify the file and line number where the error occurred.

- **Use IRB for Isolated Testing:**

  sections of your code into IRB to test them independently.

- **Leverage Built-in Debuggers:**

  Ruby's byebug gem is invaluable for stepping through code.

```ruby
```

```
gem install byebug
```

Insert byebug at critical points in your code to inspect variables and flow.

Troubleshooting Environment Setup

If your editor does not recognize Ruby syntax or IRB behaves unexpectedly, consider the following:

- **Editor Plugins:**
  Ensure that your code editor's Ruby plugins are up-to-date. Sometimes, outdated plugins can cause unexpected behavior.

- **Terminal Settings:**
  Check your terminal's PATH environment variable to ensure that Ruby and your version manager are correctly referenced.

Before-and-After Code Examples

When troubleshooting, it's often useful to compare a problematic code snippet with its corrected version. For instance, if you encounter a syntax error due to improper block termination, you might see:

Before:

```ruby

def greet
  puts "Hello, world!"
# Missing 'end'
```
After:

```ruby

def greet
  puts "Hello, world!"
end
```

These side-by-side comparisons not only resolve the error but also reinforce proper coding practices.

Conclusion & Next Steps

As we wrap up this introductory chapter, let's reflect on the journey so far and outline the steps ahead.

Recap of Key Points

In this chapter, we have:

- Explored Ruby's rich history and the philosophy that makes it unique.

- Delved into core concepts such as object orientation, dynamic typing, and the importance of developer happiness.

- Walked through setting up your development environment using tools like RVM/rbenv, your choice of code editor, and IRB.

- Created your first "Hello, World!" script and expanded to projects that cover data types, interactive menus, and even a mini calculator.

- Touched on advanced techniques and optimization strategies, setting the stage for writing clean, efficient, production-ready code.

- Addressed common troubleshooting scenarios to help you overcome potential obstacles.

Next Step

Now that you have a solid foundation in Ruby's fundamentals and environment setup, you are ready to dive deeper into more advanced topics. Here are some recommended next steps:

- **Practice Regularly:**
  Experiment with modifying the examples provided in this chapter. Try adding new features or creating variations of the projects.

- **Join the Community:**
  Engage with online forums, attend Ruby meetups, or contribute to open-source projects. The community is one of Ruby's strongest assets.

- **Explore Further Resources:**
  Look into additional tutorials, blogs, and documentation to

broaden your understanding. Consider books on Ruby and Ruby on Rails as you progress.

- **Set Personal Projects:**
  Apply what you've learned by starting a small personal project—a website, an automation script, or even a simple game. Practical experience is the best teacher.

Final Encouragement

Learning Ruby is a journey of continuous discovery. Its elegant syntax and supportive community make it a rewarding experience for beginners and professionals alike. As you move forward, remember that every programmer encounters challenges. Embrace these challenges as opportunities to deepen your understanding and refine your skills.

By mastering the setup and the basics in this chapter, you've laid the groundwork for becoming a Ruby master. The projects you've built are not just exercises—they are the first steps in a lifelong journey of coding, innovation, and problem-solving. Keep experimenting, keep learning, and most importantly, have fun with Ruby!

Chapter 2: Core Syntax and Data Types

1. Introduction

Programming languages are built upon a set of core constructs that form the basis of all coding. In Ruby, these constructs—such as strings, numbers, booleans, symbols, variables, and constants—create a framework that is at once both elegant and powerful. This chapter delves into Ruby's core syntax and data types, helping you understand how to express ideas in code with clarity and efficiency.

Ruby was designed with simplicity and readability in mind. Every element, from a basic string of text to the dynamic nature of variables, contributes to making Ruby an accessible yet robust language. Whether you are a beginner trying to get a grip on fundamental concepts, a professional refining your understanding, or a hobbyist exploring new ideas, this chapter offers detailed insights and practical examples that will empower you to write clean and effective Ruby code.

Why Core Syntax and Data Types Matter

At its heart, programming is about communicating instructions to a computer. The language's syntax—the set of rules that define the structure of your code—and its data types determine how those instructions are interpreted. In Ruby, the syntax is designed to be as natural and readable as possible, meaning that even complex operations can often be written in a manner that mirrors everyday language. Understanding these core elements is crucial because they provide the foundation upon which all other programming concepts are built. Once you have a solid grasp of strings, numbers, booleans, symbols, variables, and constants, you'll be well-equipped to tackle more advanced topics in Ruby and build real-world applications.

Key Terminology

Before we proceed, let's define some key terms:

- **String:** A sequence of characters enclosed in quotes. In Ruby, strings are used to represent text.

- **Number:** Ruby distinguishes between integers (whole numbers) and floats (numbers with decimal points).

- **Boolean:** A data type that can have only one of two values: true or false.

- **Symbol:** A lightweight, immutable identifier often used in place of strings to represent names or keys.

- **Variable:** A storage container for data. In Ruby, variables do not require explicit type declaration.

- **Constant:** Similar to variables but meant to remain unchanged throughout the program's execution.

Setting the Tone

This chapter will combine theory with practice. We'll start with detailed explanations of Ruby's data types and basic syntax, using analogies and real-world examples to make each concept accessible. Then, we'll move on to the hands-on section where you'll build a mini calculator—a practical project that reinforces what you've learned while giving you tangible, working code. Whether you're new to programming or looking to brush up on your Ruby fundamentals, the content here is designed to be both engaging and applicable to real-world scenarios.

Throughout the chapter, you will encounter clean, well-commented code snippets and visual aids (such as diagrams and flowcharts) that illustrate the flow of data and logic. The goal is to ensure that by the end of this chapter, you not only understand Ruby's core syntax and data types but also feel confident in using them to solve everyday programming challenges.

Let's dive in and explore the building blocks of Ruby that will serve as the foundation for all your future projects.

2. Core Concepts and Theory

2.1 Strings: The Heart of Text

Strings are one of the most frequently used data types in Ruby. They are sequences of characters enclosed in either single or double quotes. The choice between the two can affect how the string handles escape sequences and interpolation.

What is a String?

A string in Ruby is simply text data. For example:

```ruby
```

```ruby
message = "Hello, Ruby!"
```

Here, the variable message holds a string that can be printed, manipulated, or processed further.

Key Features and Methods

Ruby provides a wealth of built-in methods for string manipulation:

- **Concatenation:** Joining strings using the + operator or string interpolation.

- **Length:** Using .length to determine how many characters are in the string.

- **Case Conversion:** Methods like .upcase, .downcase, and .capitalize transform text to different cases.

- **Substitution and Splitting:** Methods such as .gsub for global substitution and .split for dividing a string into an array of substrings.

Real-World Analogy:

Imagine a string as a sentence in a book. Just as you can rearrange words or change the case of letters in a sentence, Ruby provides tools to alter and inspect strings effortlessly.

String Operations Diagram

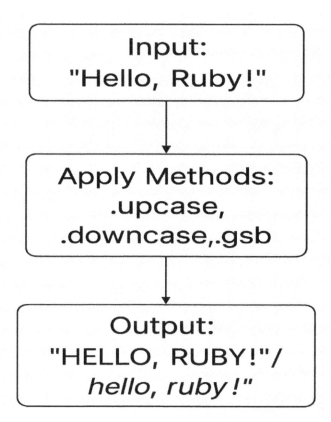

2.2 Numbers: Integers and Floats

Numbers in Ruby come in two main forms: integers and floats.

Integers

Integers are whole numbers without a fractional component:

```ruby
```

```ruby
count = 42
```

They can be used for counting, indexing, and any situation where whole numbers are required.

Floats

Floats, on the other hand, represent numbers with decimals:

```ruby
```

```ruby
price = 19.99
```

Floats are essential when precision matters, such as in financial calculations or measurements.

Arithmetic Operations

Ruby supports a variety of arithmetic operations:

- **Addition:** +

- **Subtraction:** -

- **Multiplication:** *

- **Division:** /

- **Modulo:** % (returns the remainder)

For example:

ruby

```
sum = 10 + 5          # => 15
difference = 10 - 3   # => 7
product = 4 * 5       # => 20
quotient = 20 / 4     # => 5
remainder = 20 % 3    # => 2
```

Real-World Application

Imagine using integers to count the number of items in a shopping cart and floats to calculate the total price with taxes. Understanding these numeric types is essential for both simple and complex calculations.

2.3 Booleans: True or False

Booleans are fundamental for decision-making in programming. In Ruby, the Boolean data type has two values: true and false.

Use Cases

Booleans are primarily used in conditional statements and loops to control the flow of a program.

ruby

```
is_valid = true
if is_valid
  puts "The input is valid!"
else
  puts "Please try again."
end
```

This simple conditional uses a Boolean to decide which branch of code to execute.

Comparison Operators

Ruby provides operators such as ==, !=, <, >, <=, and >= to compare values, which always return a Boolean result.

2.4 Symbols: Lightweight Identifiers

Symbols in Ruby are immutable, reusable constants represented by a colon followed by a name:

```
ruby
```

```
:username
```

They are commonly used as identifiers, keys in hashes, or for referencing method names.

Advantages of Symbols

- **Efficiency:** Symbols are stored only once in memory, making them faster for comparisons.

- **Immutability:** Once created, symbols cannot be changed, which can help prevent accidental modifications.

When to Use Symbols

Use symbols in place of strings when the identifier is meant to be used repeatedly, such as hash keys:

```ruby
person = { name: "Alice", age: 30, occupation:
:developer }
```

Here, using a symbol for :developer is both efficient and expressive.

2.5 Variables and Constants

Variables

Variables in Ruby act as containers for data. They are created dynamically without requiring explicit type declarations:

```ruby
greeting = "Hello, World!"
number = 100
```

Variables can be reassigned, making them versatile tools in any program.

Constants

Constants are similar to variables but are intended to remain unchanged once set. By convention, constants are written in all uppercase:

```ruby

PI = 3.14159
```

While Ruby does not enforce immutability strictly (it will issue a warning if you change a constant), following this convention helps maintain code clarity and integrity.

Scope and Lifetime

Understanding variable scope is crucial:

- **Local Variables:** Accessible only within the block or method where they are defined.

- **Global Variables:** Prefixed with $ and accessible from anywhere (use sparingly).

- **Instance Variables:** Prefixed with @, they belong to a specific object.

- **Class Variables:** Prefixed with @@, shared across instances of a class.

2.6 Summary of Core Concepts

At this point, you should have a solid understanding of Ruby's core data types and the syntax that brings them together. Strings, numbers, booleans, symbols, variables, and constants are the fundamental building blocks for any Ruby program. By mastering these, you set the stage for more complex constructs like control structures, methods, and object-oriented programming.

Diagram: Data Types Overview

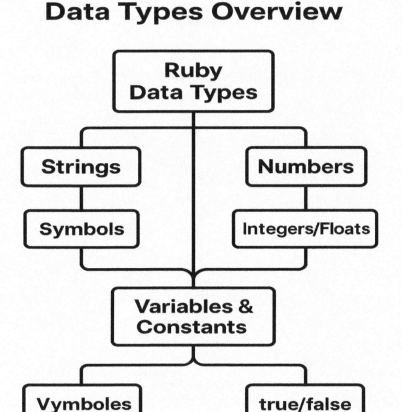

Data Types Overview

This high-level view shows how each element interrelates. As you progress, these basic elements will combine to form more sophisticated programs.

---

3. Tools and Setup

Before you can fully exploit Ruby's core syntax and data types, you must ensure that your development environment is properly configured. This section outlines the tools, platforms, and configurations that will help you get the most out of your coding experience.

3.1 Required Tools

To follow along with the exercises in this chapter, you will need:

- **Ruby Interpreter:** The core engine that executes your Ruby code.

- **A Text Editor or IDE:** Tools like Visual Studio Code, Sublime Text, or Atom that provide syntax highlighting and code assistance.

- **Terminal or Command Prompt:** To run your Ruby scripts.

- **IRB (Interactive Ruby):** A REPL environment for testing small snippets of code interactively.

3.2 Setting Up the Environment
Installing Ruby

If you have not already installed Ruby, consider using a version manager like RVM or rbenv. For example, using RVM:

1. **Install RVM:**

   Open your terminal and run:

```bash
\curl -sSL https://get.rvm.io | bash -s stable
```

2. **Install Ruby:**

   Once RVM is installed, install the latest stable version of Ruby:

```bash
rvm install ruby --latest
rvm use ruby --default
```

3. **Verify Installation:**

   Check the installation by running:

```bash
ruby -v
```

Configuring Your Editor

For example, if you choose Visual Studio Code:

1. **Install VS Code:**

    Download and install from code.visualstudio.com.

2. **Install Ruby Extensions:**

    In VS Code, navigate to the Extensions view and install a Ruby plugin (e.g., by Peng Lv).

3. **Configure Settings:**

    Edit your settings (settings.json) to enable features like auto-formatting and linting:

```json
{
  "editor.tabSize": 2,
  "files.trimTrailingWhitespace": true,
  "ruby.format": "rubocop"
}
```

Using IRB

IRB is essential for testing code snippets quickly:

- Launch **IRB** by typing irb in your terminal.

- Experiment with small code examples to verify that your setup works as expected.

4. Hands-on Examples & Projects

The true test of your understanding is applying it in practical projects. In this section, we will work through several projects that reinforce the concepts discussed so far. The projects will progress in complexity and will include clean, well-commented code, diagrams, and detailed explanations.

Project 1: Exploring Data Types with Simple Scripts

Example 1.1: String Manipulation

Create a file named string_demo.rb:

```ruby

# string_demo.rb
# This script demonstrates basic string operations in Ruby.

# Define a sample string
greeting = "Hello, Ruby World!"

# Print original string
puts "Original: #{greeting}"

# Convert to uppercase
puts "Uppercase: #{greeting.upcase}"

# Convert to lowercase
```

```ruby
puts "Lowercase: #{greeting.downcase}"

# Count the number of characters
puts "Length: #{greeting.length}"

# Replace 'Ruby' with 'Programming'
modified_greeting = greeting.gsub("Ruby",
"Programming")
puts "Modified: #{modified_greeting}"
```

Explanation:

Each method call is accompanied by a comment that explains its purpose. This script shows you how to transform and inspect strings.

Project 2: Integrating Data Types in a Combined Script

This project combines strings, numbers, booleans, and symbols in a single Ruby script to demonstrate how these elements interact.

Example 2.1: Data Types Combined

Create a file called combined_demo.rb:

```ruby
ruby

# combined_demo.rb
# Demonstrating the interaction of various data types
in Ruby.

# Define a greeting as a string
greeting = "Welcome to Ruby Demo!"
```

```ruby
# Define a count as an integer and a float value for
precision
item_count = 15
item_price = 2.99

# Calculate the total price
total_price = item_count * item_price

# Use a boolean to check if a discount applies
discount_applicable = total_price > 30

# Use a symbol to represent a category
category = :grocery

# Output the results using string interpolation
puts greeting
puts "You have #{item_count} items in the #{category}
category."
puts "Each item costs $#{item_price}. Total:
$#{total_price}."
puts "Discount applicable? #{discount_applicable}"
```

Explanation:

This script shows how to use multiple data types together. It calculates a total price, checks a condition with a Boolean, and uses a symbol to tag a category.

Visual Aid: A simple table summarizing the variables:

Variable	Type	Value
greeting	String	"Welcome to Ruby Demo!"
item_count	Integer	15
item_price	Float	2.99
total_price	Float	Calculated
discount_applicable	Boolean	true/false
category	Symbol	:grocery

5. Advanced Techniques & Optimization

As you become more comfortable with Ruby's basics, it's useful to learn some advanced techniques to write more efficient and optimized code. This section explores ways to improve your scripts by refining the use of data types and adopting best practices.

5.1 Efficient String Manipulation

When working with large volumes of text, performance can become a concern. Techniques such as using the String#<< operator for concatenation instead of the + operator can be more efficient because they modify the existing string in place. For example:

```ruby
text = ""
1000.times { text << "Ruby " }
puts text[0..50]
```

This approach minimizes the creation of new string objects and can lead to performance improvements.

5.2 Numeric Optimization

When performing numeric calculations, consider the type conversions between integers and floats. Using integers for counting and switching to floats only when necessary can save processing time. Benchmarking your code with the Benchmark module in Ruby can help identify bottlenecks:

```ruby

require 'benchmark'

Benchmark.bm do |x|
  x.report("Integer Calc:") { 100_000.times { 10 + 5 } }
  x.report("Float Calc:")   { 100_000.times { 10.to_f / 5 } }
end
```

5.3 Using Symbols for Efficiency

Since symbols are immutable and reused, prefer them over strings for identifiers that do not change. This is particularly useful when defining keys in large hashes:

```ruby
```

```
large_hash = { name: "Alice", occupation: :developer,
language: :ruby }
```

In memory-critical applications, this small optimization can make a noticeable difference.

5.4 Code Refactoring and Readability

Refactoring code for readability and efficiency is a skill that develops with practice. Consider breaking complex expressions into smaller, more manageable methods. For example, if your mini calculator grows in complexity, you might extract input validation into separate helper methods.

5.5 Advanced Data Handling Techniques

Ruby's Enumerators and lazy evaluation techniques can be very useful when processing large datasets. For example:

```
ruby
```

```
large_range = (1..1_000_000).lazy
even_numbers = large_range.select { |n| n.even? }
puts even_numbers.first(10)
```

Using lazy evaluation ensures that you don't load the entire range into memory, making your program more efficient.

Conclusion & Next Steps

As we wrap up Chapter 2, it's important to review what you've learned and how you can build upon these foundations.

Recap of Key Points

In this chapter, we explored the core syntax and data types that are the building blocks of Ruby. We began by defining essential data types such as strings, numbers, booleans, symbols, variables, and constants. We examined how each of these elements works individually and how they interact to create effective, readable code.

We delved into the theoretical underpinnings of these data types, discussing their properties and real-world applications. Whether you were learning about the mutability of strings or the efficiency of symbols, every concept was linked back to practical programming challenges.

Practical Projects

The hands-on projects—ranging from simple string manipulation scripts to a mini calculator for basic arithmetic—provided a platform to apply the concepts immediately. These projects not only reinforced the material but also offered real-world examples of how Ruby can be used to solve common problems. As you continue your journey in Ruby, consider expanding these projects by adding new features or integrating them into larger applications.

Advanced Techniques and Troubleshooting

We also touched on advanced techniques such as optimizing string concatenation, using lazy evaluation with enumerators, and profiling code performance. Coupled with a dedicated section on troubleshooting common issues, you now have a robust set of tools to debug and refine your code. Remember, encountering errors is a natural part of programming—each challenge is an opportunity to improve your skills.

Next Steps

Now that you have a solid understanding of Ruby's core syntax and data types, the next phase is to apply these fundamentals to more complex projects. Here are some recommendations:

- **Expand the Mini Calculator:** Add features such as handling multiple operations, input validation, or even a graphical user interface.

- **Experiment Further:** Create small programs that manipulate text, perform advanced calculations, or process data from external sources.

- **Join the Community:** Participate in Ruby forums, contribute to open-source projects, and continue learning through community engagement.

Final Thoughts

Understanding the basic building blocks of Ruby is crucial for any programmer. The skills you've developed in this chapter will serve as the foundation for more advanced topics such as object-oriented programming, metaprogramming, and beyond. With these fundamentals at your fingertips, you are now better prepared to explore the vast capabilities of Ruby and build innovative, high-quality code.

As you move forward, take time to revisit these concepts and experiment with them in different contexts. The more you practice, the more intuitive these data types and syntax rules will become. Your journey to becoming a Ruby master is just beginning, and the concepts covered in this chapter are stepping stones toward building powerful applications.

Chapter 3: Control Structures and Iteration

1. Introduction

Control structures and iteration are the backbone of any programming language, enabling you to dictate the flow of your programs and repeat actions until a particular condition is met. In Ruby, these structures are designed to be both powerful and readable, reflecting the language's overall philosophy of simplicity and elegance. In this chapter, we will explore conditional logic—using if, else, and case statements—and delve into the world of loops with while, until, for, and each. We will then bring these concepts together in a hands-on project where you will create a command-line guessing game.

Why Control Structures and Iteration Matter

Imagine writing a set of instructions for a robot. Without the ability to make decisions or repeat tasks, your robot could only execute one simple, fixed task. Control structures allow your code to "decide" what to do next based on current conditions, and loops let it repeat tasks until a goal is achieved. These concepts are vital in real-world programming because they enable your code to handle dynamic situations—like responding to user input, processing data, or automating repetitive tasks.

For beginners, mastering these constructs is the first step toward writing interactive and intelligent programs. Professionals will appreciate how Ruby's expressive syntax makes even complex logic easy to follow and maintain, while hobbyists can quickly see results as they build fun projects. Whether you are automating a mundane task or creating a complex game, control structures and iteration are essential tools in your programming toolkit.

Key Terminology and Concepts

Before diving in, it is important to understand several key terms:

- **Conditional Logic:** Decision-making structures that choose one block of code over another based on whether a condition is true or false.

- **if/else Statement:** The simplest form of conditional logic, where code execution is determined by a Boolean expression.

- **case Statement:** A more elegant way to handle multiple conditions or choices, similar to a switch statement in other languages.

- **Loops:** Structures that repeat a block of code multiple times. Ruby offers several types of loops: while, until, for, and the iterator each.

- **Iteration:** The process of repeating a set of instructions. Iterators in Ruby (like each) are used to traverse collections such as arrays or hashes.

Setting the Tone

This chapter is written in a clear, professional style with a focus on practical examples and real-world applications. We'll start with the theory behind conditional logic and iteration, using analogies and diagrams to simplify complex ideas. Next, we will walk through setting up the necessary tools and environment for Ruby development. Then, we'll dive into several hands-on examples that demonstrate how to use these control structures in practice. Finally, we'll create a fully functional command-line guessing game—a project that will cement your understanding of these concepts while offering an engaging, interactive experience.

By the end of this chapter, you will not only understand how to control the flow of your Ruby programs but also have built a project that demonstrates these skills in action. Let's begin our exploration into the world of control structures and iteration.

2. Core Concepts and Theory

In this section, we explore the theoretical underpinnings of Ruby's control structures and looping mechanisms. We break down conditional logic and iteration into digestible sub-sections, providing real-world analogies and code examples that illustrate each concept.

2.1 Conditional Logic: if, else, and case Statements

if/else Statements

The if statement is the simplest form of control structure. It allows you to execute a block of code only if a specific condition is true. Optionally, you can add an else clause to execute a different block if the condition is false.

Example:

```ruby

temperature = 25
if temperature > 30
  puts "It's a hot day."
else
  puts "It's a pleasant day."
end
```

Explanation:

In this example, Ruby checks whether the temperature is above 30.

If true, it prints a message about a hot day; otherwise, it prints a different message.

Real-World Analogy:

Imagine you're deciding what to wear based on the weather. If it's hot, you wear shorts; if not, you might choose jeans. The if/else statement mirrors this decision-making process.

elsif

Ruby also supports the elsif keyword for checking multiple conditions in a sequence.

```ruby
score = 85
if score >= 90
  puts "Grade: A"
elsif score >= 80
  puts "Grade: B"
elsif score >= 70
  puts "Grade: C"
else
  puts "Grade: D or below"
end
```

Explanation:

Here, Ruby evaluates several conditions in order. As soon as one condition is met, the corresponding code block is executed.

case Statements

When dealing with multiple discrete values, the case statement can simplify your code.

```ruby
day = "Monday"
case day
when "Saturday", "Sunday"
  puts "It's the weekend!"
when "Friday"
  puts "Almost the weekend!"
else
  puts "It's a weekday."
end
```

Explanation:

The case statement compares the value of day against multiple conditions. It is particularly useful when you have many alternatives.

Flowchart of Conditional Logic

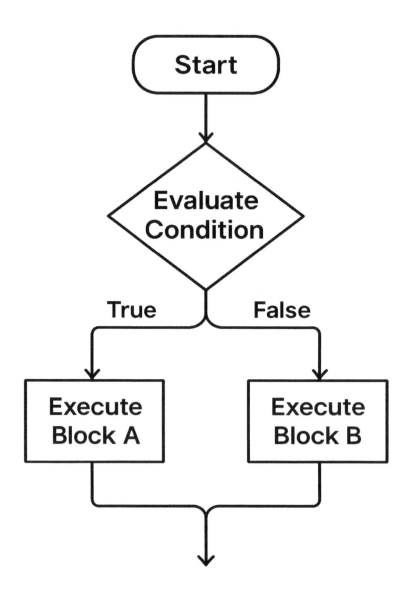

2.2 Iteration: Loops and Iterators

Iteration allows you to repeat a block of code. Ruby provides several looping mechanisms.

while Loop

The while loop executes a block of code as long as a condition remains true.

ruby

```ruby
count = 1
while count <= 5
  puts "Count is #{count}"
  count += 1
end
```

Explanation:

This loop will print the value of count from 1 to 5. The loop stops when the condition becomes false.

until Loop

The until loop is the opposite of while: it executes until the condition is true.

ruby

```ruby
count = 1
until count > 5
  puts "Count is #{count}"
```

```
  count += 1
end
```

Explanation:

Here, the loop continues until count becomes greater than 5.

for Loop

The for loop iterates over a range or collection.

```
ruby
```

```
for number in 1..5
  puts "Number: #{number}"
end
```

Explanation:

This loop iterates over the range 1 to 5 and prints each number.

each Iterator

The each method is Ruby's most common iterator and is used with collections like arrays.

```
ruby
```

```
[1, 2, 3, 4, 5].each do |number|
  puts "Number: #{number}"
end
```

Explanation:

This block iterates over each element of the array, assigning it to the variable number.

Real-World Analogy:

Imagine you have a stack of postcards to mail. Using a loop is like picking one postcard at a time, mailing it, and then moving to the next until none remain.

2.3 Combining Conditional Logic with Iteration

The true power of control structures and iteration comes when they are combined. For example, you might iterate over a list of numbers and only process those that meet a certain condition:

ruby

```
numbers = [1, 2, 3, 4, 5, 6, 7, 8, 9, 10]
numbers.each do |n|
  if n.even?
    puts "#{n} is even."
  else
    puts "#{n} is odd."
  end
end
```

Explanation:

For each number in the array, the code checks whether it is even or odd and prints the appropriate message.

2.4 Theoretical Insights and Best Practices

Readability and Simplicity

Ruby's syntax is designed for readability. When writing control structures, clear indentation and simple expressions help maintain clarity. Avoid overly complex conditions in a single statement; instead, break them into smaller, understandable parts.

Efficiency Considerations

While loops are powerful, always consider whether a particular loop is the most efficient option. For example, iterators such as each are often preferred for their clarity and built-in methods.

Common Patterns in Ruby

- **Guard Clauses:** Instead of nesting conditions deeply, use guard clauses to handle exceptional cases early.

ruby

```ruby
def process_number(n)
  return "Invalid" if n.nil?
  n.even? ? "Even" : "Odd"
end
```

- **Ternary Operator:** For simple conditions, the ternary operator can make your code more concise.

ruby

```ruby
result = (score > 50) ? "Pass" : "Fail"
```

Real-World Example: Filtering Data

Consider a scenario where you need to filter a list of orders based on their status. Using a combination of iteration and conditional logic, you can efficiently separate orders that are "shipped" from those that are "pending." This not only simplifies your code but also makes it easy to maintain and extend.

3. Tools and Setup

Before diving into our hands-on examples and project, let's review the tools and setup required to work with Ruby's control structures and iteration. This section ensures your development environment is ready and that you have the necessary resources to follow along.

3.1 Required Tools

To work with Ruby effectively, ensure you have the following:

- **Ruby Interpreter:** Make sure Ruby is installed on your machine (use RVM or rbenv if needed).

- **Text Editor or IDE:** Visual Studio Code, Sublime Text, or Atom are excellent choices.

- **Terminal or Command Prompt:** To run your Ruby scripts and test your code interactively.

- **IRB (Interactive Ruby):** For quick experimentation with code snippets.

3.2 Setting Up Your Environment
Installing Ruby

If Ruby is not installed yet, follow these steps (using **RVM** as an example):

1. **Install RVM:**

bash

```
\curl -sSL https://get.rvm.io | bash -s stable
```

2. **Install Ruby:**

bash

```
rvm install ruby --latest
rvm use ruby --default
```

3. **Verify Installation:**

bash

```
ruby -v
```

Configuring Your Code Editor

For Visual Studio Code:

1. **Install VS Code:** Download from code.visualstudio.com.

2. **Install Ruby Extensions:** Search for and install popular Ruby extensions.

3. **Configure Settings:** Adjust settings (e.g., tab size, auto-formatting) in your settings.json.

```json
json

{

  "editor.tabSize": 2,
  "files.trimTrailingWhitespace": true,
  "ruby.format": "rubocop"
}
```

Using IRB

IRB is a great tool to test small snippets of code:

- Launch IRB by typing irb in your terminal.

- Experiment with conditionals and loops before integrating them into larger scripts.

---

4. Hands-on Examples & Projects

This section is dedicated to practical examples and projects. We begin with simple exercises that reinforce the theory of conditionals and loops, then build up to a full command-line guessing game. Each example includes clean, well-commented code and diagrams to help visualize the process.

4.1 Example 1: Conditional Statements in Action
Exercise: Evaluate a Student's Grade

Create a file named grade_evaluator.rb:

```ruby
# grade_evaluator.rb
# This script evaluates a student's score and outputs
a grade.

score = 82

if score >= 90
  grade = "A"
elsif score >= 80
  grade = "B"
elsif score >= 70
  grade = "C"
elsif score >= 60
  grade = "D"
else
  grade = "F"
end

puts "Student score: #{score} -> Grade: #{grade}"
```

Explanation:

This script uses an if/elsif/else structure to determine a student's grade based on their score.

4.2 Example 2: Looping Over a Collection
Exercise: Print Numbers and Identify Even/Odd

Create a file named even_odd.rb:

```ruby
# even_odd.rb
# This script iterates over an array of numbers and
prints whether each number is even or odd.

numbers = [1, 2, 3, 4, 5, 6, 7, 8, 9, 10]
numbers.each do |number|
  if number.even?
    puts "#{number} is even."
  else
    puts "#{number} is odd."
  end
end
```

Explanation:

This example demonstrates how to iterate over an array with the each iterator, applying a conditional check for evenness.

4.3 Example 3: Using while and until Loops
Exercise: Count Down from 10 Using while and until

Create a file named countdown.rb:

```ruby
```

```ruby
# countdown.rb
# Demonstrates countdown using while and until loops.

# Using while
count = 10
while count > 0
  puts "Countdown (while): #{count}"
  count -= 1
end

puts "Liftoff using while loop!"

# Reset count for until loop
count = 10
until count == 0
  puts "Countdown (until): #{count}"
  count -= 1
end

puts "Liftoff using until loop!"
```

Explanation:

This script uses both while and until loops to count down from 10, showing the slight difference in how each loop condition is written.

5. Advanced Techniques & Optimization

Now that you have a solid grasp of basic control structures and loops, let's explore some advanced techniques and optimizations to write cleaner, more efficient Ruby code.

5.1 Optimizing Conditional Statements
Guard Clauses

Guard clauses allow you to exit a method early if a condition is met, reducing nested logic.

ruby

```ruby
def check_number(n)
  return "Invalid" if n.nil?
  n > 0 ? "Positive" : "Non-positive"
end
```

Benefit:

This approach makes your code easier to read by handling exceptional cases immediately.

Ternary Operator

For simple conditions, the ternary operator provides a concise alternative:

ruby

```ruby
result = (score >= 50) ? "Pass" : "Fail"
```

Trade-Off:

While concise, use the ternary operator sparingly to avoid sacrificing clarity.

5.2 Advanced Loop Techniques
Using Iterators with Collections

Ruby's built-in iterators (e.g., each, map, select) provide powerful tools for processing collections in a functional style.

ruby

```
numbers = (1..10).to_a
squared_numbers = numbers.map { |n| n * n }
even_numbers = numbers.select { |n| n.even? }
```

Explanation:

- **map:** Transforms each element in the collection.

- **select:** Filters elements based on a condition.

Lazy Enumerators

For large datasets, Ruby's lazy enumerators delay computation until needed, saving memory.

ruby

```
large_range = (1..1_000_000).lazy
```

```ruby
first_ten = large_range.select(&:even?).first(10)
puts first_ten.inspect
```

Explanation:

Lazy evaluation means only the necessary elements are processed, optimizing performance.

5.3 Performance Considerations

Profiling Your Code

Use Ruby's Benchmark module to measure and optimize loop performance:

```ruby
ruby

require 'benchmark'

Benchmark.bm do |x|
  x.report("Loop:") { 100_000.times { 1 + 1 } }
end
```

Explanation:

Benchmarking helps identify bottlenecks, allowing you to refine your control structures for better performance.

Minimizing Redundant Checks

When iterating, avoid recalculating values inside the loop if they remain constant. For instance, compute a complex condition once before entering the loop rather than within each iteration.

5.4 Best Practices for Advanced Control Structures

- **Keep Conditions Simple:** Break down complex conditions into helper methods.

- **Use Meaningful Variable Names:** This increases readability and maintainability.

- **Refactor Repeated Patterns:** Extract common patterns into methods or iterators.

- **Leverage Ruby's Enumerable Methods:** They often offer more expressive and concise ways to manipulate collections.

Conclusion & Next Steps

Recap of Key Points

In this chapter, we explored the essential control structures and iteration techniques in Ruby. We began by examining conditional logic—covering if/else, elsif, and case statements—and learned how these tools allow our programs to make decisions based on dynamic conditions. We then dove into various looping mechanisms such as while, until, for, and the each iterator, learning how to repeat operations efficiently. The hands-on examples, including the creation of a command-line guessing game, demonstrated how these concepts work together in a real-world project.

Project Recap: The Guessing Game

The command-line guessing game project brought together conditional logic and loops in an engaging, interactive way. You learned to:

- Generate a random number.

- Use a loop to repeatedly prompt for user input.

- Validate input and provide feedback using if/elsif/else structures.

- Enhance the game with input validation and a replay option.

Advanced Techniques and Optimization

We also touched on advanced techniques—such as guard clauses, the ternary operator, and lazy enumerators—to optimize your code. Profiling with the Benchmark module and refactoring complex conditionals are key skills for writing efficient, maintainable Ruby code.

Troubleshooting and Continued Learning

Debugging is an inevitable part of programming. We covered common pitfalls like off-by-one errors, infinite loops, and misplaced end statements, and provided strategies to resolve them. As you continue your Ruby journey, remember that every bug is an opportunity to deepen your understanding.

Next Steps

Now that you have mastered control structures and iteration, you are ready to apply these techniques to more advanced projects. Here are some recommended next steps:

- **Expand Your Projects:** Enhance the guessing game by adding difficulty levels or integrating a scoring system.

- **Practice Regularly:** Write small programs that make use of conditionals and loops to solve everyday problems.

- **Explore More Ruby Features:** Investigate Ruby's enumerable methods further, and learn how to combine them with control structures for powerful data manipulation.

- **Join the Community:** Engage with Ruby forums, participate in coding challenges, and collaborate on open-source projects to broaden your skills.

Final Thoughts

Control structures and iteration are fundamental building blocks in programming. By mastering these concepts in Ruby, you have taken an important step toward writing robust, interactive, and efficient code. The principles and techniques discussed in this chapter will serve as the foundation for more complex topics in later chapters. Whether you are a beginner, professional, or hobbyist, the ability to control program flow and iterate effectively is key to solving problems and building innovative applications.

As you move forward, revisit these examples, experiment with modifications, and challenge yourself with new projects. Your journey to becoming a proficient Ruby developer continues—with each loop, conditional, and project, you are honing your craft.

Chapter 4: Methods, Blocks, and Functional Tools

1. Introduction

Programming in Ruby is much more than simply writing sequential lines of code. It is about encapsulating functionality, reusing code, and building small, elegant pieces of functionality that can be composed into larger, powerful applications. In Ruby, methods, blocks, and functional tools—such as procs and lambdas—play a vital role in achieving these goals. They help in organizing code, improving readability, and allowing developers to solve problems in a modular and reusable way.

Methods in Ruby let you define a named block of code that you can call repeatedly, optionally with parameters and return values. They form the foundation of code abstraction and reuse. Beyond methods, Ruby introduces blocks—a powerful, unnamed piece of code that can be passed to methods—and further functional constructs like procs and lambdas, which are objects representing blocks of code. These tools allow you to write code in a functional style, creating flexible and dynamic behavior in your programs.

This chapter explores these essential elements in depth. We will start by discussing the theory behind methods, how to define them, pass parameters, and return values. We will then delve into blocks and their close relatives: procs and lambdas. Each concept is explained using analogies and practical examples to make them accessible to beginners while also offering deeper insights for advanced readers.

In the latter half of the chapter, you will roll up your sleeves and build a hands-on project: a text formatter that applies user-defined rules to format input text. This project will illustrate how methods, blocks, and functional tools can work together to create powerful, reusable functionality. By the end of this chapter, you will have a thorough understanding of Ruby's approach to encapsulation and functional programming, enabling you to write cleaner, more modular code.

As you read, you'll notice that our approach is both detailed and practical. We want you to understand not only how to use these features but also why they are important in real-world programming scenarios. Whether you are new to Ruby or an experienced developer looking to refine your skills, mastering methods and blocks will elevate the way you write code.

2. Core Concepts and Theory

In this section, we explore the theoretical foundation behind methods, blocks, and functional tools in Ruby. We start by explaining methods: what they are, how to define them, and how to work with parameters and return values. Then, we examine blocks, procs, and lambdas, comparing their similarities and differences. Throughout, we use real-world analogies and code examples to illustrate these ideas.

2.1 Methods: The Building Blocks of Abstraction
Defining Methods

A method in Ruby is like a mini-program that you can call by name. It allows you to encapsulate a set of instructions into a reusable unit. Methods are defined using the def keyword and closed with the end keyword.

Example:

```ruby

def greet
  puts "Hello, Ruby Enthusiast!"
end
```
When you call greet, the message is printed to the screen. This simple example shows the basic syntax of a method.

Parameters and Arguments

Methods often require information to operate. Parameters are placeholders defined in the method's signature, and when the method is called, you pass arguments to fill these parameters.

Example:

```ruby
ruby
```

```ruby
def greet_user(name)
  puts "Hello, #{name}! Welcome to Ruby."
end
```

```ruby
greet_user("Alice")
```
Here, the method greet_user takes one parameter (name), and when we call it with "Alice", it prints a personalized greeting.

Real-World Analogy:

Imagine a coffee machine where you can choose the type of coffee you want. The machine (method) is programmed to make coffee based on the type (parameter) you select (argument).

Return Values

Every method in Ruby can return a value using the return keyword, though Ruby will automatically return the last evaluated expression if no explicit return is given.

Example:

```ruby
ruby
```

```
def add(a, b)
  a + b
end
```

```
sum = add(5, 7)   # sum now holds the value 12
```

In this case, the add method calculates the sum and returns it.

Key Concepts:

- **Encapsulation:** Methods encapsulate behavior into reusable components.

- **Abstraction:** By defining methods, you hide complex logic behind simple calls.

- **Reusability:** Methods allow you to write a piece of code once and use it throughout your application.

2.2 Blocks: Anonymous Code Chunks

A block in Ruby is a piece of code enclosed between do...end or curly braces {...} that can be passed to methods. Blocks are not objects on their own but can be converted into procs.

Using yield

The yield keyword allows a method to execute a block passed to it. This is one of Ruby's most powerful features.

Example:

```ruby

def perform_task
  puts "Before yield"
  yield if block_given?
  puts "After yield"
end

perform_task { puts "Inside the block!" }
```

Explanation:

In this example, perform_task executes the block between its output statements. If no block is given, block_given? prevents an error.

Real-World Analogy:

Think of yield as a call to an assistant: "After I finish my current task, please do this for me." The block is the assistant's task that is executed at the right moment.

Blocks vs. Methods

Blocks can be passed as temporary chunks of code without naming them. They are useful for one-off operations that don't need to persist as separate methods.

Procs and Lambdas

Procs and lambdas are objects that encapsulate blocks of code, allowing you to store, pass, and execute them later.

Proc Example:

```ruby
ruby


my_proc = Proc.new { |x| puts "Value: #{x}" }
my_proc.call(10)
Lambda Example:
ruby


my_lambda = ->(x) { puts "Lambda Value: #{x}" }
my_lambda.call(20)
```

Differences:

- **Lambda:** Checks the number of arguments, and returns control differently.

- **Proc:** More lenient with arguments and returns control to the calling method when done.

Key Concepts:

- **Reusability:** Procs and lambdas allow you to reuse blocks of code.

- **Higher-Order Functions:** They enable passing code as data, a hallmark of functional programming.

- **Flexibility:** Using these functional tools, you can build more abstract and reusable code structures.

2.3 Functional Tools in Ruby

Ruby supports a functional programming style with methods like map, select, and reduce. These methods, combined with blocks, allow you to process collections in a concise and readable way.

Example:

```ruby
```

```ruby
numbers = [1, 2, 3, 4, 5]
squared = numbers.map { |n| n * n }
puts squared.inspect  # Outputs: [1, 4, 9, 16, 25]
```

Explanation:

The map method applies the block to each element in the array and returns a new array with the results.

Real-World Analogy:

Imagine you have a basket of apples and you want to wash each one. Instead of washing them one by one with manual instructions, you set up an automated process (map) that washes every apple in the basket.

---

3. Tools and Setup

Before you start building projects that leverage these functional tools, you need to ensure your development environment is properly configured. This section walks you through the necessary tools and step-by-step instructions for setting up your environment.

3.1 Required Tools

To work with Ruby's methods, blocks, and functional tools, you will need:

- **Ruby Interpreter:** The core engine for executing Ruby code.

- **Version Manager (RVM or rbenv):** To manage and switch between Ruby versions.

- **Text Editor or IDE:** Visual Studio Code, Sublime Text, or Atom, with Ruby syntax support.

- **Terminal or Command Prompt:** To run Ruby scripts and test your code.

- **IRB (Interactive Ruby):** A REPL environment for experimenting with small code snippets.

3.2 Installing Ruby and a Version Manager

If Ruby isn't already installed, use RVM or rbenv. Below are the steps for using RVM:

1. **Install RVM:**

bash

```
\curl -sSL https://get.rvm.io | bash -s stable
```

2. **Install Ruby:**

```bash
bash
```

```bash
rvm install ruby --latest
rvm use ruby --default
```

3. **Verify Installation:**

```bash
bash
```

```bash
ruby -v
```

3.3 Configuring Your Code Editor

For Visual Studio Code:

1. **Download and Install VS Code:**

   Get it from code.visualstudio.com.

2. **Install Ruby Extensions:**

   Search for Ruby extensions (such as the one by Peng Lv) in the Extensions marketplace.

3. **Configure Settings:**

   Open your settings.json file and add configuration options:

```json
json
```

```json
{
  "editor.tabSize": 2,
  "files.trimTrailingWhitespace": true,
  "ruby.format": "rubocop"
```

```
}
```

3.4 Using IRB for Rapid Prototyping

IRB (Interactive Ruby) is a valuable tool for testing methods, blocks, and procs quickly:

- Open your terminal and type irb.

- Experiment by defining small methods and passing blocks.

- For example:

```ruby
ruby


def demo
  yield if block_given?
end

demo { puts "Hello from IRB!" }
```

4. Hands-on Examples & Projects

In this section, we bring theory to practice with a series of hands-on examples. We start with small code snippets that demonstrate how to define methods, use blocks, and work with procs and lambdas. Then, we will combine all these elements in a comprehensive project: a text formatter with user-defined rules.

4.1 Example 1: Defining and Using Methods
Exercise: Basic Method Definition

Create a file named basic_method.rb:

ruby

```
# basic_method.rb
# Demonstrates how to define and call a simple
method.

def say_hello(name)
  "Hello, #{name}!"
end

puts say_hello("Ruby Developer")
```

Explanation:

This method takes a single parameter and returns a greeting string. The code is clean, with proper indentation and comments explaining each step.

4.2 Example 2: Using yield with Blocks
Exercise: Method with Yield

Create a file named yield_demo.rb:

ruby

```
# yield_demo.rb
```

```
# Demonstrates the use of yield to execute a block
within a method.

def perform_action
  puts "Before yield"
  yield if block_given?
  puts "After yield"
end

perform_action { puts "Hello from the block!" }
```

Explanation:

The method perform_action calls yield to execute the block passed to it. This pattern is common in Ruby for creating flexible methods that accept custom behavior.

4.3 Example 3: Procs and Lambdas in Action

Exercise: Creating and Calling Procs and Lambdas

Create a file named proc_lambda_demo.rb:

```
ruby

# proc_lambda_demo.rb
# Demonstrates the creation and use of procs and
lambdas.

# Define a proc
greeting_proc = Proc.new { |name| "Hi, #{name} from
Proc!" }
```

```ruby
puts greeting_proc.call("Alice")

# Define a lambda
greeting_lambda = ->(name) { "Hi, #{name} from
Lambda!" }
puts greeting_lambda.call("Bob")
```

Explanation:

This example contrasts procs and lambdas, highlighting differences in how they handle arguments and return values.

---

5. Advanced Techniques & Optimization

In this section, we dive deeper into advanced strategies for working with methods, blocks, and functional tools. We focus on writing efficient, maintainable, and reusable code.

5.1 Optimizing Method Design

Refactoring Methods for Clarity

Large methods can often be broken down into smaller helper methods. This increases readability and makes testing easier.

Before:

```ruby
ruby

def process_text(text)
  text = text.strip
```

```ruby
  text = text.gsub(/\s+/, ' ')
  text = text.split.map(&:capitalize).join(' ')
  text
end
```

After (Refactored):
ruby

```ruby
def clean_whitespace(text)
  text.gsub(/\s+/, ' ').strip
end

def capitalize_words(text)
  text.split.map(&:capitalize).join(' ')
end

def process_text(text)
  text = clean_whitespace(text)
  capitalize_words(text)
end
```

Explanation:

Breaking the method into smaller parts enhances readability and reusability.

Parameter Default Values and Keyword Arguments

Ruby allows you to define default values for parameters and use keyword arguments to improve clarity.

Example:

```ruby

def greet_user(name:, greeting: "Hello")
  "#{greeting}, #{name}!"
end


puts greet_user(name: "Alice")              # Outputs:
Hello, Alice!
puts greet_user(name: "Bob", greeting: "Hi")   #
Outputs: Hi, Bob!
```

Benefit:

This makes the method calls more self-documenting and flexible.

5.2 Advanced Block Techniques
Capturing Blocks as Procs

Sometimes you want to capture the block passed to a method as a proc for later use. You can do this by converting the block using the &block syntax.

Example:

```ruby

def process_collection(collection, &block)
  collection.map(&block)
end


result = process_collection([1, 2, 3]) { |n| n * 2 }
puts result.inspect  # Outputs: [2, 4, 6]
```

Explanation:

Here, the block is captured as a proc and passed to map, demonstrating seamless integration between blocks and methods.

Advanced Lambdas and Procs

Understanding the differences between lambdas and procs is key to advanced functional programming in Ruby. Lambdas check the number of arguments and use their own return behavior, while procs are more flexible but less strict.

Example Comparison:

ruby

```
def test_lambda
  my_lambda = ->(x) { return x * 2 }
  result = my_lambda.call(10)
  puts "Lambda result: #{result}"
end

def test_proc
  my_proc = Proc.new { |x| return x * 2 }
  result = my_proc.call(10)
  puts "This line is never reached in test_proc"
end

test_lambda    # Outputs: Lambda result: 20
```

```
test_proc       # Returns from the entire method
immediately
```

Explanation:

The above examples illustrate how a lambda's return only exits the lambda, whereas a proc's return exits the containing method.

5.3 Functional Programming Patterns

Ruby's functional tools allow you to use patterns like higher-order functions, currying, and partial application. These patterns help create flexible, composable code.

Higher-Order Functions

A higher-order function is one that takes other functions (or procs) as arguments or returns them as results.

Example:

```ruby
ruby

def apply_twice(proc_obj, value)
  proc_obj.call(proc_obj.call(value))
end

double = ->(x) { x * 2 }
puts apply_twice(double, 5)   # Outputs: 20
```

Benefit:

This pattern increases code reusability and abstraction.

Currying and Partial Application

Currying transforms a method that takes multiple arguments into a chain of methods each taking one argument.

Example:

```ruby
ruby

def multiply(a, b)
  a * b
end

curried_multiply = method(:multiply).curry
double = curried_multiply.call(2)
puts double.call(10)   # Outputs: 20
```

Explanation:

This technique allows you to create specialized functions from general ones.

5.4 Performance Optimization

While methods and blocks provide great flexibility, they also incur overhead. Profiling your code with tools like Ruby's Benchmark module can help identify performance bottlenecks.

Example Benchmark:

```ruby
ruby

require 'benchmark'

Benchmark.bm do |x|
```

```
  x.report("Method call:") { 100_000.times { add(1,
2) } }
  x.report("Inline addition:") { 100_000.times { 1 +
2 } }
end
```

Explanation:

Compare the performance of repeated method calls versus inline operations to understand the trade-offs.

5.5 Best Practices for Advanced Functional Tools

- **Keep Blocks Simple:** Complex logic in blocks can be hard to debug. When needed, extract logic into methods.

- **Use Clear Naming:** When capturing blocks as procs, give them descriptive names.

- **Avoid Excessive Nesting:** Deeply nested blocks and procs can make code difficult to follow.

- **Document Behavior:** Clearly comment on the intended behavior of methods that accept blocks or procs, especially if they involve early returns or non-obvious control flow.

Conclusion & Next Steps

Recap of Key Points

In this chapter, we delved into Ruby's approach to methods, blocks, and functional tools. We learned how to define methods, pass parameters, and return values, and we explored the power of blocks to dynamically inject code. We examined procs and lambdas, understanding their differences and how they enhance code flexibility. Through practical examples and the comprehensive project—a text formatter with user-defined rules—we saw these concepts in action.

Project Recap: Text Formatter

The text formatter project demonstrated how to combine multiple functional tools:

- **Methods** were used to encapsulate formatting logic.

- **Blocks** allowed dynamic behavior by letting users define formatting rules.

- **Procs and Lambdas** provided reusable and flexible formatting rules.

- **Composition:** The formatters were composed in a pipeline to transform text step by step.

This project not only solidified your understanding but also gave you a practical tool that can be extended and customized.

Advanced Techniques and Optimization

We discussed advanced strategies, such as refactoring methods for clarity, using keyword arguments, and optimizing block usage. We explored functional programming patterns like higher-order functions and currying. These techniques help you write more modular, efficient, and maintainable code, making your applications more robust and scalable.

Troubleshooting and Continued Learning

Every developer encounters challenges. We reviewed common pitfalls such as incorrect parameter counts and unintended return behaviors, along with practical debugging strategies. Embracing these challenges as opportunities to learn will help you become a more skilled Ruby developer.

Next Steps

As you move forward, consider the following:

- **Expand the Text Formatter:** Add new formatting rules such as converting to uppercase, inserting prefixes/suffixes, or even integrating natural language processing for more complex transformations.

- **Explore Ruby's Enumerable Module:** Experiment with other functional tools and iterators to process collections more effectively.

- **Practice Modular Design:** Refactor your code to break it into smaller, testable methods.

- **Engage with the Ruby Community:** Join forums, contribute to open-source projects, and participate in coding challenges to further your understanding and refine your skills.

Final Thoughts

Understanding methods, blocks, and functional tools is essential to writing elegant and maintainable Ruby code. These concepts not only help you encapsulate logic and reduce redundancy, but they also empower you to write code that is flexible and expressive. As you continue your journey in Ruby programming, revisit these concepts, experiment with them, and incorporate best practices into every project you build.

The tools and techniques presented in this chapter are stepping stones to more advanced programming paradigms. With a solid grasp of these ideas, you are well-equipped to tackle more complex challenges and build powerful, reusable code components. Keep exploring, experimenting, and building—the possibilities are endless.

Chapter 5: Object-Oriented Programming Fundamentals

1. Introduction

Object-Oriented Programming (OOP) is a paradigm that has transformed the way we design and build software. In Ruby, OOP is not just an add-on feature—it is woven into the fabric of the language. With its elegant syntax and natural approach to modeling real-world entities, Ruby makes it straightforward to create classes and objects that mirror our everyday experiences.

Imagine trying to manage a complex system like a social networking site or a banking application without the ability to group related data and behavior together. Classes allow you to bundle state and behavior, while objects are the real-life instantiations of those blueprints. In Ruby, understanding how to define classes, differentiate between instance and class methods, and apply core OOP concepts such as encapsulation, inheritance, and polymorphism is crucial for writing maintainable, reusable, and scalable code.

This chapter explores these fundamental ideas in detail. We start by defining what classes and objects are, how they are declared, and the difference between instance methods (which belong to individual objects) and class methods (which belong to the class itself). We then move into the core principles of OOP: encapsulation (hiding internal details), inheritance (extending behavior), and polymorphism (treating different objects through the same interface). Throughout, we use real-world analogies—such as comparing a class to a blueprint for a house or an object to the actual house—to ground abstract ideas in everyday experience.

Our practical example in this chapter is a simple 'User' class. By modeling a user with basic attributes (such as name, email, and age) and methods that perform common tasks (like updating information or greeting the user), you will see OOP principles in action. This example is designed to be accessible for beginners while also offering insights and best practices that seasoned professionals will appreciate.

Whether you are new to programming or an experienced developer looking to refine your skills, understanding Ruby's OOP features will empower you to create better software. As you progress through this chapter, you'll learn not only how to design and implement classes and objects but also how to think in an object-oriented way—

an approach that leads to clearer, more organized, and more maintainable code.

In the following sections, we provide a deep dive into the theory behind OOP, offer step-by-step instructions on setting up your environment, walk through hands-on examples and projects, and discuss advanced techniques and troubleshooting strategies. By the end of this chapter, you will have a comprehensive understanding of Ruby's object-oriented features and be ready to apply these concepts in real-world projects.

---

2. Core Concepts and Theory

In this section, we explore the underlying concepts of object-oriented programming as implemented in Ruby. We discuss classes and objects in detail, explain the differences between instance methods and class methods, and introduce key OOP principles like encapsulation, inheritance, and polymorphism. Our goal is to break down each concept with clear definitions, analogies, and code examples.

2.1 Classes and Objects
What Is a Class?

A class is a blueprint for creating objects. It defines a set of attributes (data) and methods (behaviors) that the objects created from it will have. In Ruby, you define a class using the class keyword followed by the class name and a block of code ending with end.

Example:

```ruby
ruby
```

```ruby
class User
  # Class body goes here
end
```

In this simple example, the class User is declared without any attributes or methods yet. Think of a class as a detailed blueprint for a house—while it doesn't represent an actual home, it specifies what every house built from that blueprint should have.

Creating Objects (Instances)

Once a class is defined, you can create objects (instances) of that class using the new method.

Example:

```ruby
ruby
```

```ruby
user1 = User.new
```

Here, user1 is an instance of the User class. Each object created from a class is independent, with its own state.

2.2 Instance Methods vs. Class Methods

Instance Methods

Instance methods are defined to operate on individual objects. They typically manipulate or display the state of an instance.

Example:

```ruby
```

```ruby
class User
  def greet
    puts "Hello! Welcome to our application."
  end
end

user1 = User.new
user1.greet  # Calls the instance method 'greet'
```

Explanation:

The greet method is defined inside the class and is available on each instance of User. When called, it performs an action specific to that object.

Class Methods

Class methods are defined on the class itself rather than on its instances. They are often used for functionality that is relevant to the class as a whole.

Example:

```ruby
```

```
class User
  def self.total_users
    # For example, return the count of user instances
(if tracked)
    100  # Placeholder value
  end
end

puts User.total_users  # Calls the class method
'total_users'
```

Explanation:

Using the self. prefix, the total_users method is declared as a class method. You call it directly on the class without needing to instantiate an object.

Real-World Analogy:

Consider a car manufacturing plant. The blueprint (class) defines how to build a car, and each car (object) has its own characteristics. However, a class method might be like a report generated by the factory that shows the total number of cars produced.

2.3 OOP Concepts
Encapsulation

Encapsulation is the principle of bundling data (attributes) and methods that work on that data within a single unit (class). It helps hide the internal state of an object and exposes only what is necessary.

Example:

```ruby
ruby

class User
  def initialize(name, email)
    @name = name
    @email = email
  end

  def display_info
    "User: #{@name}, Email: #{@email}"
  end
end

user1 = User.new("Alice", "alice@example.com")
puts user1.display_info
```

Explanation:

Here, @name and @email are instance variables that are encapsulated within the User class. The method display_info is the public interface that exposes the user's information.

Inheritance

Inheritance allows one class (a subclass) to inherit attributes and methods from another class (a superclass). This supports code reuse and a hierarchical relationship between classes.

Example:

ruby

```ruby
class Person
  def initialize(name)
    @name = name
  end

  def greet
    "Hello, I'm #{@name}."
  end
end

class User < Person
  def initialize(name, email)
    super(name)
    @email = email
  end

  def display_info
    "#{greet} My email is #{@email}."
  end
end

user1 = User.new("Bob", "bob@example.com")
puts user1.display_info
```

Explanation:

The User class inherits from Person and gains access to the greet method. It extends the functionality by adding an email attribute and a new method.

Polymorphism

Polymorphism means that different classes can implement the same method in different ways. It allows objects of different types to be treated uniformly based on a common interface.

Example:

ruby

```ruby
class Admin < User
  def display_info
    "#{greet} I have administrative privileges."
  end
end

def print_user_info(user)
  puts user.display_info
end

user = User.new("Carol", "carol@example.com")
admin = Admin.new("Dave", "dave@example.com")
print_user_info(user)    # Calls User#display_info
print_user_info(admin)   # Calls Admin#display_info
(polymorphism in action)
```

Explanation:

Both User and Admin implement display_info, but in different ways. The function print_user_info treats both objects uniformly.

---

3. Tools and Setup

Before diving into coding examples, you need a properly configured development environment. This section explains the tools required to work with Ruby's OOP features, along with step-by-step setup instructions.

3.1 Required Tools

To work effectively with Ruby's object-oriented programming, you will need:

- **Ruby Interpreter:** The engine that executes Ruby code.

- **Version Manager (RVM or rbenv):** For managing different Ruby versions.

- **Text Editor or IDE:** Options like Visual Studio Code, Sublime Text, or Atom with Ruby syntax support.

- **Terminal or Command Prompt:** For running Ruby scripts.

- **IRB (Interactive Ruby):** A REPL environment for experimenting with Ruby code.

3.2 Installing Ruby

If Ruby isn't installed, you can use a version manager. Here's an example with RVM:

1. **Install RVM:**

```bash

\curl -sSL https://get.rvm.io | bash -s stable
```

2. **Install the Latest Ruby Version:**

```bash

rvm install ruby --latest
rvm use ruby --default
```

3. **Verify Installation:**

```bash

ruby -v
```

3.3 Configuring Your Code Editor

For Visual Studio Code:

1. **Download and Install VS Code:**

   Visit code.visualstudio.com to download.

2. **Install Ruby Extensions:**

   Open the Extensions view (Ctrl+Shift+X or Cmd+Shift+X) and search for "Ruby" by Peng Lv or similar.

3. **Adjust Settings:**

Modify your settings.json to include:

```json

{

  "editor.tabSize": 2,
  "files.trimTrailingWhitespace": true,
  "ruby.format": "rubocop"
}
```

3.4 Using IRB for Prototyping

IRB is a quick way to test small snippets of code. To launch IRB, open your terminal and type:

```bash

irb
```

Experiment by defining small classes and invoking methods to verify that your environment is correctly set up.

---

4. Hands-on Examples & Projects

This section is dedicated to hands-on examples that bring the theory of object-oriented programming to life. We begin with simple class definitions and move through creating a practical 'User' class with attributes and methods. Finally, we build a small project that models real-world behavior.

4.1 Example 1: Defining a Simple Class
Exercise: Create a Basic User Class

Create a file named user_basic.rb:

ruby

```
# user_basic.rb
# A simple User class demonstrating basic OOP in
Ruby.

class User
  # Constructor: initializes a new user with a name
and email.
  def initialize(name, email)
    @name = name
    @email = email
  end

  # Instance method: returns a greeting message.
  def greet
    "Hello, #{@name}! Welcome to our platform."
  end
end

# Create an instance of User.
user1 = User.new("Alice", "alice@example.com")
puts user1.greet  # Outputs: Hello, Alice! Welcome to
our platform.
```

Explanation:

This code defines a User class with an initializer (the initialize method) that sets up the user's name and email, and an instance method greet that returns a welcome message.

A diagram showing the flow:

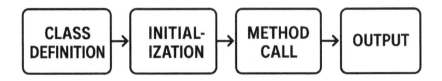

4.2 Example 2: Instance vs. Class Methods
Exercise: Differentiating Methods

Create a file named user_methods.rb:

```ruby

# user_methods.rb
# Demonstrates instance methods and a class method in
the User class.

class User
  # Class variable to track total users.
  @@total_users = 0

  # Constructor: increments user count.
  def initialize(name, email)
```

```ruby
    @name = name
    @email = email
    @@total_users += 1
  end

  # Instance method: returns user info.
  def info
    "Name: #{@name}, Email: #{@email}"
  end

  # Class method: returns total number of users.
  def self.total_users
    @@total_users
  end
end

# Create multiple users.
user1 = User.new("Bob", "bob@example.com")
user2 = User.new("Carol", "carol@example.com")

puts user1.info        # Outputs user1's information.
puts user2.info        # Outputs user2's information.
puts User.total_users # Outputs: 2
```

Explanation:

Here, instance methods operate on each object, while the class method total_users tracks a class-level variable.

Conclusion & Next Steps

Recap of Key Points

In this chapter, we explored the fundamentals of object-oriented programming in Ruby. We defined classes and objects, clarified the difference between instance and class methods, and delved into the core OOP concepts of encapsulation, inheritance, and polymorphism. Through our examples—from a simple User class to a comprehensive user management system—we saw how to model real-world entities using Ruby's OOP features.

Reflecting on the 'User' Class Example

The 'User' class served as a practical example to illustrate:

- **Encapsulation:** Hiding internal state and exposing behavior through methods.

- **Inheritance:** Building a hierarchy that reuses and extends functionality.

- **Polymorphism:** Allowing methods to behave differently depending on the object type.

Advanced Techniques and Best Practices

We also discussed advanced techniques such as refactoring methods, leveraging mixins, optimizing object creation, and using performance profiling. Embracing these best practices will help you write more modular, efficient, and maintainable code.

Troubleshooting and Continued Learning

Every programmer encounters challenges. By using the troubleshooting strategies outlined in this chapter—such as testing in IRB, reading error messages carefully, and refactoring complex code—you will be better equipped to diagnose and fix issues in your OOP designs. Continued practice, combined with engagement in the Ruby community, will further refine your skills.

Next Steps

As you move forward, consider the following:

- **Expand Your Projects:** Enhance your User Management System by adding features like authentication or role-based access.

- **Dive Deeper into OOP:** Explore design patterns (such as Singleton, Observer, or Factory) to solve common programming problems.

- **Learn from Open Source:** Study popular Ruby projects and libraries to see how experienced developers apply OOP principles.

- **Practice Regularly:** Build small applications that model real-world entities—every project is an opportunity to improve your OOP skills.

Final Thoughts

Object-oriented programming is a powerful paradigm that, when mastered, will enable you to write robust and flexible code. The techniques covered in this chapter—from defining classes and methods to understanding inheritance and polymorphism—form the backbone of modern software development in Ruby. As you continue your journey, keep experimenting with new ideas, refactor your code for clarity, and always look for ways to improve the design of your applications.

Your newfound understanding of Ruby's object-oriented features is not just theoretical—it is a practical toolkit you can apply to build real-world solutions. Embrace these concepts, and let them inspire you to write clean, maintainable, and scalable code.

Chapter 6: Advanced OOP: Modules, Mixins, and Error Handling

---

1. Introduction

Object-oriented programming (OOP) in Ruby goes far beyond the basics of classes and inheritance. As your applications grow in size and complexity, you need techniques that help you share functionality without duplicating code, organize your design in a modular fashion, and build robust programs that can gracefully recover from errors. In this chapter, we explore advanced topics in Ruby's OOP world: modules, mixins, and error handling.

Modules are one of Ruby's most powerful features. They allow you to group related methods, constants, and even classes into a single unit. By including a module as a mixin into a class, you can share behavior across multiple classes without resorting to deep inheritance hierarchies. This "composition over inheritance" approach leads to cleaner, more maintainable code and gives you the flexibility to reuse functionality in diverse parts of your application.

Alongside modules and mixins, robust error handling is essential in production code. No matter how carefully you design your application, errors and exceptions will occur. Ruby provides an elegant way to catch and handle these exceptions using begin-rescue-ensure blocks. With proper error handling, your applications can manage unexpected conditions—whether it's a missing file, invalid user input, or a network timeout—without crashing, thereby providing a smoother experience for users.

This chapter is designed for beginners who are now ready to tackle more advanced topics, professionals seeking to enhance their code's robustness, and hobbyists interested in applying best practices in their projects. We will start by discussing modules and mixins and then move on to exception handling. Finally, we'll integrate these concepts into a hands-on project—a library management system that not only models books and borrowers but also gracefully handles errors.

Throughout this chapter, you will see real-world analogies that explain abstract concepts in everyday terms. For example, imagine a module as a toolbox filled with useful tools. Rather than each craftsman reinventing the wheel, they share the same tools to perform common tasks. Similarly, mixins let different classes share the same functionality without forcing an "is-a" relationship. And just as a skilled driver uses safety measures to avoid accidents, error handling in your code ensures that unexpected situations are managed properly.

By the end of this chapter, you will have a deep understanding of how modules and mixins allow for elegant code reuse and how exception handling can make your application robust and user-friendly. You'll also have built a fully functional library management system that demonstrates these advanced OOP techniques in a practical, real-world scenario. With clear, well-commented code examples and visual aids throughout, this chapter will empower you to write scalable, maintainable Ruby applications that gracefully handle error conditions.

2. Core Concepts and Theory

In this section, we dive into the underlying theory of modules, mixins, and error handling in Ruby. We'll cover the following topics:

2.1 Modules & Mixins
What Are Modules?

A module in Ruby is a collection of methods, constants, and class variables. Unlike classes, modules cannot be instantiated. Instead, they are used as namespaces or as a mechanism to share reusable functionality across classes. Think of a module as a container of methods—a toolkit that any class can borrow from.

```ruby
Example:
ruby


module Greetings
  def say_hello
    "Hello!"
  end

  def say_goodbye
    "Goodbye!"
  end
end
```

In this example, the Greetings module defines two methods that can be mixed into classes.

Using Modules as Namespaces

Modules can also act as namespaces, helping to avoid name collisions in large projects.

```ruby
ruby


module LibrarySystem
  class Book
    attr_accessor :title, :author
    def initialize(title, author)
```

```ruby
    @title = title
    @author = author
  end
 end
end


book = LibrarySystem::Book.new("1984", "George
Orwell")
puts book.title  # Outputs: 1984
```

Explanation:

Here, the LibrarySystem module wraps the Book class. This not only organizes the code but also prevents conflicts with other classes named Book.

Mixins: Sharing Functionality

Mixins allow you to include the functionality of a module within a class. When you use the include keyword, all the module's methods become available as instance methods of that class.

Example:

```ruby
ruby


class User
  include Greetings

  def initialize(name)
    @name = name
```

```
  end

  def introduce
    "#{say_hello} I am #{@name}."
  end
end

user = User.new("Alice")
puts user.introduce  # Outputs: Hello! I am Alice.
```

Real-World Analogy:

Imagine a mixin as a shared recipe. Instead of each chef writing their own recipe for a dish, they all refer to a single recipe (module) that they include in their cooking routine.

Benefits of Modules and Mixins

- **Code Reuse:** Write a piece of functionality once and use it in multiple classes.

- **Organization:** Keep your codebase modular and well-organized.

- **Flexibility:** Avoid rigid inheritance hierarchies by sharing behavior through modules.

2.2 Exception Handling

Understanding Exceptions

Exceptions are events that disrupt the normal flow of execution. In Ruby, exceptions are objects that represent errors or unexpected conditions. When an error occurs, Ruby raises an exception.

Example:

```ruby

raise "Something went wrong!"
```

This simple line stops the program and displays an error message.

The Begin-Rescue-Ensure Construct

Ruby provides a clear syntax for handling exceptions using begin-rescue-ensure blocks.

Basic Syntax:

```ruby

begin
  # Code that may raise an exception
rescue StandardError => e
  # Code that runs if an exception is raised
ensure
  # Code that always runs, regardless of whether an
exception occurred
end
```

Explanation:

- **begin:** Wraps the code that might fail.

- **rescue:** Catches exceptions and allows you to handle them.

- **ensure:** Contains cleanup code that executes no matter what.

Example:

```ruby
ruby
```

```ruby
begin
  file = File.open("non_existent_file.txt", "r")
  # Process file
rescue Errno::ENOENT => e
  puts "File not found: #{e.message}"
ensure
  file.close if file
end
```

In this example, if the file doesn't exist, the rescue block catches the exception and prints an error message. The ensure block makes sure that the file is closed if it was opened.

Custom Exceptions

Ruby allows you to define your own exception classes by subclassing StandardError.

Example:

```ruby
ruby
```

```ruby
class LibraryError < StandardError; end
```

```ruby
def find_book(title)
  raise LibraryError, "Book not found: #{title}" if
title.empty?
  # Return book details
end
```

Explanation:

Custom exceptions help create more descriptive and specific error messages that are easier to debug and handle.

2.3 Combining Modules and Error Handling

Modules can be used not only for sharing functionality but also for encapsulating error-handling logic. You can define a module that wraps methods in error handling, making it easier to maintain consistent error handling across your application.

Example:

```
ruby
```

```ruby
module SafeExecution
  def safely
    yield
  rescue StandardError => e
    puts "An error occurred: #{e.message}"
  end
end

class Task
  include SafeExecution
```

```
def perform
  safely do
    # Code that might raise an error
    raise "Unexpected error!"
  end
 end
end
```

```
Task.new.perform   # Outputs: An error occurred:
Unexpected error!
```

Explanation:

This module defines a safely method that wraps any block of code with begin-rescue logic. Classes including this module can call safely to ensure that errors are caught and handled uniformly.

2.4 Key Terminology

- **Module:** A collection of methods, constants, and other definitions that cannot be instantiated.

- **Mixin:** A technique to share functionality among classes using modules.

- **Exception:** An object that represents an error or unexpected event.

- **Begin-Rescue-Ensure:** Ruby's construct for handling exceptions gracefully.

- **Custom Exception:** A user-defined exception class that provides more specific error information.

2.5 Real-World Analogies

Consider a module as a shared utility belt used by different professionals—a firefighter, a mechanic, and an electrician might all have access to the same high-quality toolset. Mixins allow these different "classes" to share the same tools without forcing them into the same family hierarchy. Similarly, error handling in your application is like having a safety net. When something goes wrong— whether it's a system malfunction or a miscommunication—a well-designed error-handling strategy catches the issue and prevents a complete collapse.

---

3. Tools and Setup

Before you begin writing advanced OOP code in Ruby, you must ensure that your development environment is set up correctly. This section provides a step-by-step guide to installing Ruby, configuring your text editor or IDE, and verifying your setup with IRB.

3.1 Required Tools

To work effectively with modules, mixins, and error handling in Ruby, you will need:

- **Ruby Interpreter:** The engine that executes your Ruby code.

- **Version Manager (RVM or rbenv):** For managing different Ruby versions.

- **Text Editor or IDE:** Visual Studio Code, Sublime Text, or Atom, configured for Ruby development.

- **Terminal or Command Prompt:** For running Ruby scripts and testing code.

- **IRB (Interactive Ruby):** A REPL environment for experimenting with Ruby code snippets.

3.2 Installing Ruby with RVM

If Ruby is not yet installed on your machine, using **RVM** is one of the simplest ways to get started.

Step-by-Step Installation:

1. **Install RVM:**

bash

```
\curl -sSL https://get.rvm.io | bash -s stable
```

Visual Aid: A screenshot of the terminal during **RVM** installation.

2. **Install the Latest Ruby Version:**

bash

```
rvm install ruby --latest
rvm use ruby --default
```

3. **Verify Installation:**

```bash
bash
```

```bash
ruby -v
```

3.3 Configuring Your Text Editor

For Visual Studio Code users:

1. **Download and Install VS Code:**

   Visit code.visualstudio.com and follow the instructions.

2. **Install Ruby Extensions:**

   Open the Extensions view (Ctrl+Shift+X or Cmd+Shift+X) and search for "Ruby" (e.g., Ruby by Peng Lv).

3. **Configure Settings:**

   Add the following settings in your settings.json:

```json
json
```

```json
{
  "editor.tabSize": 2,
  "files.trimTrailingWhitespace": true,
  "ruby.format": "rubocop"
}
```

3.4 Using IRB for Testing

IRB (Interactive Ruby) is ideal for quickly testing small pieces of code:

- Open your terminal.

- Type irb and press Enter.

- Experiment with defining modules and invoking methods.

Example:

```ruby
ruby

module TestModule
  def test_method
    "Module method executed."
  end
end

class Dummy
  include TestModule
end

d = Dummy.new
puts d.test_method  # Should output: Module method executed.
```

---

4. Hands-on Examples & Projects

This section presents practical examples that illustrate the use of modules, mixins, and error handling. We start with smaller examples and build up to a comprehensive project—a library management system that gracefully handles errors.

4.1 Example 1: Creating a Module for Shared Functionality

Exercise: Define a Utility Module

Create a file named utilities.rb:

ruby

```ruby
# utilities.rb
# A module that provides common utility methods for
our application.

module Utilities
  def self.format_date(date)
    date.strftime("%B %d, %Y")
  end

  def self.strip_whitespace(text)
    text.gsub(/\s+/, ' ').strip
  end
end

# Demonstrate module usage.
puts Utilities.format_date(Time.now)
puts Utilities.strip_whitespace("  This   is   a
test.   ")
```

Explanation:

The Utilities module defines two class methods for formatting dates and cleaning up whitespace. These can be used throughout your application without duplication.

4.2 Example 2: Mixing in Modules for Reusable Behavior

Exercise: Create a Mixin for Error Logging

Create a file named error_logger.rb:

ruby

```ruby
# error_logger.rb
# A module that provides error logging functionality.

module ErrorLogger
  def log_error(error)
    puts "ERROR: #{error.class} - #{error.message}"
    # In a real application, you might write this to
a log file.
  end
end

# Example usage in a class.
class FileProcessor
  include ErrorLogger

  def process(file_path)
```

```
begin
  content = File.read(file_path)
  puts "File content loaded successfully."
rescue StandardError => e
  log_error(e)
end
    end
  end
end


processor = FileProcessor.new
processor.process("non_existent_file.txt")
```

Explanation:

The ErrorLogger module provides a method to log errors. The FileProcessor class includes this module, so it can call log_error when handling exceptions.

Conclusion & Next Steps

Recap of Key Points

In this chapter, we explored advanced object-oriented programming techniques in Ruby. We delved into the use of modules and mixins as powerful tools for sharing functionality across classes, which promotes a modular and DRY codebase. We then examined robust exception handling using begin-rescue-ensure blocks and learned how to create custom exceptions for more descriptive error management. The comprehensive project—a library management system—illustrated how these techniques can be combined to build a real-world application that gracefully handles errors while offering rich functionality.

Reflecting on the Library Management System Project

The library management system project demonstrated:

- **Modular Design:** How to use modules to encapsulate utility methods and error logging.

- **Mixins:** How to share functionality among different parts of your application without resorting to deep inheritance hierarchies.

- **Error Handling:** How to catch and handle exceptions gracefully to ensure that your application remains stable even when unexpected issues occur.

Advanced Techniques and Best Practices

We also covered advanced techniques such as refining modules for reuse, using custom exceptions, and applying performance optimizations. These practices not only improve the robustness of your code but also make it more maintainable and scalable for future growth.

Troubleshooting and Continued Learning

Encountering errors is inevitable in software development. The strategies discussed in this chapter—such as using IRB for testing, inserting debug statements, and writing comprehensive unit tests—will help you diagnose and resolve issues efficiently. Embrace troubleshooting as a valuable skill that will improve your overall programming proficiency.

Next Steps

To build on the knowledge from this chapter:

- **Expand the Library System:** Add features like book reservations, user authentication, or overdue notifications.

- **Explore Further:** Investigate more advanced Ruby topics such as metaprogramming, design patterns, and concurrent programming.

- **Join the Community:** Engage with Ruby forums, contribute to open-source projects, and participate in code reviews to continuously refine your skills.

- **Read and Research:** Consider further reading on Ruby best practices and advanced object-oriented design.

Final Thoughts

Advanced OOP concepts like modules, mixins, and error handling are key to writing clean, robust, and maintainable Ruby code. By mastering these techniques, you not only improve your code's quality but also empower yourself to build complex applications that are resilient in the face of errors. The strategies and best practices outlined in this chapter provide a solid foundation for tackling real-world programming challenges, ensuring that your applications remain reliable and user-friendly.

As you continue your journey in Ruby, keep experimenting with these advanced concepts. Every new project is an opportunity to refine your approach, optimize your code, and push the boundaries of what you can achieve with Ruby's elegant object-oriented features.

Chapter 7: Writing Clean, Maintainable, and Testable Code

1. Introduction

In today's fast-paced software development environment, writing code that is clean, maintainable, and testable is not just a desirable quality—it's a necessity. As projects grow in complexity and teams expand, ensuring that the codebase remains readable, modular, and robust can mean the difference between a successful launch and a prolonged period of debugging and refactoring. In Ruby, best practices, style guides, and testing frameworks have evolved to help developers achieve these goals. This chapter provides a comprehensive look at how you can write code that stands the test of time.

At its core, clean code is code that is easy to read and understand. Maintainable code can be easily modified and extended by you or by others in the future. Testable code is structured in such a way that automated tests can verify its correctness, reducing the risk of regression when changes are made. Throughout this chapter, we'll discuss key concepts and best practices for achieving these ideals.

We begin by exploring Ruby style guides—collections of recommendations that help maintain consistency and clarity across a codebase. Tools like RuboCop enforce these style rules automatically, catching deviations before they become problematic. Next, we dive into refactoring techniques: strategies for reorganizing your code without changing its external behavior. Refactoring not only improves readability but also reduces technical debt over time.

Testing is the final pillar of a maintainable codebase. We'll introduce you to two popular testing frameworks—RSpec and Minitest—and discuss test-driven development (TDD), a methodology that encourages writing tests before code. By integrating testing into your development workflow, you ensure that your code behaves as expected and can be refactored with confidence.

This chapter is designed for developers at all levels. Beginners will gain an introduction to the principles of clean code and learn why these practices matter, while professionals will find advanced tips and techniques to optimize their workflow. Hobbyists, too, will appreciate the practical examples that demonstrate how to apply these concepts in real-world scenarios.

Throughout the chapter, you will encounter clear definitions of key terms such as "refactoring," "style guide," and "TDD." Real-world analogies—like comparing a codebase to a well-organized library—help illustrate why these practices are essential. Our goal is to equip you with the knowledge and tools to not only write better code but also to communicate your intent clearly to fellow developers.

By the end of this chapter, you will understand how to leverage style guides and automated linters, refactor legacy code for clarity, and write comprehensive tests that safeguard your work. We will also walk you through an exercise where you refactor an existing project and add tests to it—demonstrating the tangible benefits of these practices.

Let's dive in and explore how to elevate your Ruby code to a professional standard that is both clean and resilient.

---

2. Core Concepts and Theory

In this section, we break down the theoretical foundations of writing clean, maintainable, and testable code. We start with style guides and the role of RuboCop, then discuss refactoring, and finally move to testing principles and TDD.

2.1 Style Guides and RuboCop

The Importance of Style Guides

A style guide is a set of conventions that standardize code formatting and practices across a project. In Ruby, style guides cover everything from indentation and naming conventions to more nuanced practices like the preferred way to chain method calls. Consistency in code style is crucial because it makes the code easier to read and understand, regardless of who wrote it.

Real-World Analogy:

Imagine reading a book where every chapter is written in a different font, uses different punctuation, and follows no logical structure. Such inconsistency would make it difficult to comprehend the overall narrative. Similarly, a consistent code style makes it easier for team members to quickly grasp and contribute to a project.

Popular Ruby Style Guides

The Ruby community has developed several style guides, including the widely accepted "Ruby Style Guide" found on GitHub. This guide covers best practices in code formatting, naming, and even certain patterns to avoid. Following a well-established style guide ensures that your code meets community standards and can be easily understood by other Ruby developers.

RuboCop: Automated Style Enforcement

RuboCop is a static code analyzer that enforces the Ruby style guide. It automatically checks your code for style violations and can even auto-correct many issues.

Example RuboCop Configuration (in .rubocop.yml):

```yaml
AllCops:
  TargetRubyVersion: 3.0
  Exclude:
    - 'db/schema.rb'

Layout/LineLength:
  Max: 100

Style/StringLiterals:
  EnforcedStyle: double_quotes
```

Explanation:

This configuration file sets the target Ruby version, excludes specific files from analysis, and enforces a maximum line length and the use of double quotes for string literals.

```
$ rubocop
Inspecting 10 files
10 files inspected, 10 offenses detected
Auto-correcting offenses...
10 offenses corrected

app/controllers/users_controller.rb:3:1  Trailing
whitespace detected
**R/helpers/application_helper.rb:7:5  Style/String-
Prefer single-quoted strings when you don't need str
interpolation or escape sequences
***/models/user.b:8:13  Style/Documentation  Missing
top-level documditrtion comment  Layout/IndentationW
contfig/aplication.rb:5:1  Sty(e/FrozenStringLiteral
lib/tasks/sample.rake:18:9  Style/NumericLiterals  U
underscore(_) as thousands separator and separate ev
B digits with them
spec/models/post_spec.rb:28:11  Style/BlockDelimiter
spec/support/authentication_helpers.rb:12:3  Method
too many lines  Lint/AmbiguousBlock Association  Par
the param 'delete(:destroy, id: article.id) {....}' t
```

2.2 Refactoring: Improving Code Readability and Maintainability

What Is Refactoring?

Refactoring is the process of restructuring existing code without changing its external behavior. It aims to improve the internal structure of the code, making it more understandable, flexible, and easier to modify. Common refactoring techniques include extracting methods, renaming variables, and eliminating duplicate code.

Example Before and After:

Before Refactoring:

ruby

```ruby
def process_order(order)
  # Process items in order
  order.items.each do |item|
    if item.price > 100
      puts "High value item: #{item.name}"
    else
      puts "Regular item: #{item.name}"
    end
  end
end
```

After Refactoring:

ruby

```ruby
def process_order(order)
  order.items.each { |item| process_item(item) }
end

def process_item(item)
  if expensive?(item)
    puts "High value item: #{item.name}"
```

```
  else
    puts "Regular item: #{item.name}"
  end
end

def expensive?(item)
  item.price > 100
end
```

Explanation:

By extracting the logic into separate methods (process_item and expensive?), the code becomes easier to read and test. Each method now has a single responsibility, adhering to the Single Responsibility Principle (SRP).

Benefits of Refactoring

- **Improved Readability:** Smaller, well-named methods are easier to understand.

- **Reduced Complexity:** Breaking down complex logic into discrete methods simplifies reasoning about the code.

- **Enhanced Testability:** Smaller methods can be unit tested in isolation, leading to a more reliable codebase.

- **Easier Maintenance:** A modular codebase is easier to modify and extend without unintended side effects.

Real-World Analogy:

Think of refactoring like organizing a cluttered workshop. By grouping related tools together and labeling them clearly, you can find what you need quickly and work more efficiently.

2.3 Testing and Test-Driven Development (TDD)
The Importance of Testing

Testing is the practice of verifying that your code works as expected. Automated tests serve as a safety net, catching regressions when changes are made and ensuring that each component behaves correctly. In Ruby, testing frameworks such as RSpec and Minitest help automate this process.

Benefits of Automated Testing:

- **Confidence in Code Changes:** Tests alert you if a change breaks existing functionality.

- **Documentation:** Tests serve as live documentation of how your code is supposed to work.

- **Refactoring Support:** With a comprehensive test suite, you can refactor your code with the assurance that its behavior remains unchanged.

Introduction to RSpec and Minitest

RSpec is a behavior-driven development (BDD) framework that allows you to write tests in a human-readable format. Its expressive syntax makes it easy to describe the expected behavior of your code.

Example RSpec Test:

```ruby
# spec/user_spec.rb
require 'user'

RSpec.describe User do
  describe "#greet" do
    it "returns a greeting message with the user's name" do
      user = User.new("Alice", "alice@example.com", 30)
      expect(user.greet).to eq("Hello, Alice! You are 30 years old.")
    end
  end
end
```

Explanation:

This test checks that the greet method of the User class returns the expected greeting message. The syntax is intuitive and closely resembles natural language.

Minitest is another testing framework that comes bundled with Ruby. It is lightweight and straightforward, making it a good choice for smaller projects or when you want to avoid additional dependencies.

Example Minitest Test:

ruby

```ruby
# test/user_test.rb
require "minitest/autorun"
require_relative "user"

class UserTest < Minitest::Test
  def test_greet
    user = User.new("Bob", "bob@example.com", 25)
    assert_equal "Hello, Bob! You are 25 years old.",
user.greet
  end
end
```

Explanation:

This test defines a class inheriting from Minitest::Test and uses assertions to verify that the greet method works as expected.

Test-Driven Development (TDD)

Test-driven development is a methodology in which you write tests before writing the actual code. TDD follows a simple cycle:

1. **Write a Test:** Define what you expect your code to do.

2. **Run the Test:** It should fail initially since the functionality isn't implemented yet.

3. **Write the Code:** Implement the functionality to pass the test.

4. **Refactor:** Clean up the code while keeping the tests green.

5. **Repeat.**

Real-World Analogy:

Imagine planning a building by first drawing detailed blueprints (tests) before you start construction (code). The blueprints ensure that every element of the building meets the desired specifications.

---

3. Tools and Setup

Before you can write and test clean, maintainable code, you need the right tools and an optimized development environment. This section outlines the necessary software and provides step-by-step instructions for setting up your Ruby environment.

3.1 Required Tools

To work on writing maintainable and testable Ruby code, you will need:

- **Ruby Interpreter:** The engine that runs your Ruby code.

- **Version Manager (RVM or rbenv):** For managing Ruby versions.

- **Text Editor or IDE:** Visual Studio Code, Sublime Text, or Atom with Ruby plugins.

- **Terminal or Command Prompt:** For running Ruby scripts.

- **RuboCop:** For automated style checking.

- **RSpec and/or Minitest:** For writing tests.

- **IRB:** For quickly testing code snippets.

3.2 Installing Ruby with a Version Manager

If you have not installed Ruby, you can use RVM as follows:

1. **Install RVM:**

```bash
```

```bash
\curl -sSL https://get.rvm.io | bash -s stable
```

Visual Aid: A screenshot of terminal output during RVM installation.

2. **Install the Latest Ruby Version:**

```bash
```

```bash
rvm install ruby --latest
rvm use ruby --default
```

3. Verify Installation:

```bash
ruby -v
```

3.3 Setting Up Your Text Editor

For Visual Studio Code:

1. **Download and Install VS Code:**

   Visit code.visualstudio.com to download.

2. **Install Ruby Extensions:**

   In the Extensions view (Ctrl+Shift+X), search for "Ruby" (e.g., Ruby by Peng Lv) and install it.

3. **Configure Your Editor:**

   Add the following settings to your settings.json:

```json
{
  "editor.tabSize": 2,
  "files.trimTrailingWhitespace": true,
  "ruby.format": "rubocop"
}
```

3.4 Installing and Configuring RuboCop

RuboCop is essential for enforcing style guidelines. Install it by running:

```bash
gem install rubocop
```

Create a configuration file (.rubocop.yml) in your project directory:

```yaml
AllCops:
  TargetRubyVersion: 3.0
Layout/LineLength:
  Max: 100
Style/StringLiterals:
  EnforcedStyle: double_quotes
```

Visual Aid: A screenshot of RuboCop output in the terminal.

3.5 Installing Testing Frameworks

For RSpec, add it to your Gemfile:

```ruby
group :test do
  gem 'rspec'
end
```

Then run:

```bash
bundle install
rspec --init
```

For Minitest, no additional installation is needed as it comes with Ruby.

3.6 Using IRB for Quick Testing

IRB is useful for experimenting with code fragments. Open IRB in your terminal:

```bash
irb
```

Test a simple method:

```ruby
def greet(name)
  "Hello, #{name}!"
end
puts greet("Rubyist")
```

---

4. Hands-on Examples & Projects

This section provides practical examples to reinforce the concepts discussed above. We start with small examples that illustrate style, refactoring, and testing, and then work through a comprehensive exercise: refactoring an existing project and adding tests.

4.1 Example 1: Enforcing Style with RuboCop

Create a file named example_style.rb:

```ruby

# example_style.rb
# A simple Ruby script that intentionally violates
some style rules.

def  greet( name )
  puts 'Hello, ' + name + "!"
end

greet( "Alice" )
Run RuboCop:
```

```bash

rubocop example_style.rb
```

Explanation:

RuboCop will report issues such as extra spaces and the use of single quotes where double quotes might be preferred, according to our configuration. Auto-correct by running:

```bash

rubocop -a example_style.rb
```

4.2 Example 2: Refactoring for Readability

Consider a legacy method that processes orders:

```ruby

# legacy_order_processor.rb
```

```ruby
def process_order(order)
  # Validate order
  if order[:items].nil? || order[:items].empty?
    return "No items to process"
  end

  total = 0
  order[:items].each do |item|
    if item[:price] && item[:quantity]
      total += item[:price] * item[:quantity]
    else
      return "Invalid item in order"
    end
  end

  "Order total is $#{total}"
end
```

Refactored Version:

ruby

```ruby
# order_processor.rb
def valid_order?(order)
  order[:items] && !order[:items].empty?
end

def calculate_total(order)
  order[:items].reduce(0) do |sum, item|
    sum + item[:price].to_f * item[:quantity].to_i
  end
```

```
end

def process_order(order)
  return "No items to process" unless
valid_order?(order)

  total = calculate_total(order)
  "Order total is $#{total}"
end
```

Explanation:

By extracting helper methods (valid_order? and calculate_total), the code is more modular and easier to maintain.

Conclusion & Next Steps

Recap of Key Points

In this chapter, we explored the critical practices of writing clean, maintainable, and testable Ruby code. We began by examining style guides and the role of RuboCop in enforcing a consistent code style. We then delved into refactoring techniques that help you break down complex code into modular, understandable pieces. Finally, we introduced testing methodologies with RSpec and Minitest and discussed the principles of test-driven development (TDD).

Reflecting on the Exercise

Our hands-on exercise—refactoring an existing project and adding tests—demonstrated the tangible benefits of these practices. By applying style guidelines, extracting helper methods, and writing comprehensive tests, you transformed a legacy codebase into a cleaner, more maintainable, and reliable application.

Advanced Techniques and Optimization

We also discussed advanced refactoring strategies, performance considerations, and best practices for ensuring that your code remains efficient as it grows. Embracing these techniques not only improves the quality of your code but also makes it easier for others to contribute and maintain it over time.

Troubleshooting and Continued Learning

Every developer encounters challenges when refactoring and testing code. The troubleshooting strategies outlined in this chapter—such as using debugging tools, reading error messages carefully, and writing tests before refactoring—are essential skills that will serve you well in your ongoing projects. As you continue to refine your coding practices, consider incorporating regular code reviews and automated testing into your workflow.

Next Steps

To build on the knowledge gained in this chapter:

- **Expand Your Projects:** Continue refactoring your existing projects and add more comprehensive tests.

- **Explore Advanced Testing:** Look into integration and end-to-end testing, and experiment with continuous integration (CI) tools.

- **Engage with the Community:** Participate in open-source projects and code reviews to share and learn best practices.

- **Keep Learning:** Read additional resources such as *"Eloquent Ruby"* and *"Practical Object-Oriented Design in Ruby"* to deepen your understanding.

Final Thoughts

Writing clean, maintainable, and testable code is a lifelong pursuit. The practices discussed in this chapter are not just about following rules—they are about creating a codebase that is a pleasure to work with and that can evolve gracefully over time. By adhering to style guides, refactoring thoughtfully, and embracing a test-driven approach, you empower yourself and your team to build robust, scalable applications.

Remember, the key to improvement is continuous practice and learning. Refactor your code regularly, write tests for new features, and always strive for clarity in your implementations. As you continue your journey, you will find that the effort invested in writing clean code pays off many times over in reduced bugs, easier collaboration, and a codebase that stands the test of time.

Chapter 8: Metaprogramming and DSLs

1. Introduction

In the evolving world of Ruby programming, there comes a point when basic object-oriented concepts and procedural code are no longer enough to express the complexity or elegance you envision for your application. This is where metaprogramming and domain-specific languages (DSLs) come into play. Metaprogramming is the art of writing code that writes or modifies other code at runtime, making your programs more flexible, concise, and expressive. DSLs take this concept further by providing a specialized language tailored to a particular problem domain, enabling you to describe solutions in a way that closely mirrors natural language or domain-specific terminology.

Why should you care about metaprogramming and DSLs? For beginners, these concepts open a door into a more dynamic and flexible style of coding that can reduce redundancy and simplify complex tasks. For professionals, metaprogramming is a powerful tool that can greatly reduce boilerplate code and help enforce conventions across large codebases. Hobbyists, too, will enjoy the creative possibilities these techniques offer—they allow you to build mini-languages that can be fun to experiment with while solving real-world problems in a concise manner.

In this chapter, we will start by discussing the theoretical underpinnings of metaprogramming in Ruby. We will explore how Ruby's dynamic nature lets you create methods on the fly using tools such as method_missing and define_method. Then, we'll transition into the world of DSLs—discussing why and how you would build a DSL for configuration or other specialized tasks. Our approach is hands-on and example-driven. You'll see code snippets that clearly demonstrate each metaprogramming technique, along with diagrams that illustrate how dynamic method creation and DSL parsing work under the hood.

We will then culminate with a practical project: developing a DSL for a hypothetical web service. This project will illustrate how to design a configuration language that allows users to specify routes, middleware, and settings in a clear, declarative style. By integrating metaprogramming techniques with DSL construction, you will learn to build flexible systems that can be easily extended or modified without changing the underlying core code.

Throughout this chapter, we define key terminology such as "metaprogramming," "DSL," "method_missing," and "define_method" to ensure clarity. Real-world analogies—like comparing metaprogramming to a chef who can create new recipes on the fly, or a DSL to a specialized toolkit for a mechanic—are used to bridge the gap between abstract concepts and practical understanding.

By the end of this chapter, you'll understand not only how metaprogramming works in Ruby but also how to harness it to create your own mini-languages that make your code more expressive, maintainable, and fun. Whether you're looking to cut down on repetitive code or create a clean API for your application, the skills you acquire here will open up new ways of thinking about and solving programming challenges.

2. Core Concepts and Theory

In this section, we delve deeply into the theory behind Ruby's metaprogramming capabilities and the creation of DSLs. We break down the concepts into digestible sub-sections, each accompanied by practical code examples and analogies.

2.1 Metaprogramming in Ruby
What Is Metaprogramming?

Metaprogramming is the technique of writing code that can inspect, modify, or even create code at runtime. In Ruby, everything is an object—including classes and methods—which means you can manipulate these objects dynamically. This flexibility allows you to write generic, reusable code that adapts based on context.

Real-World Analogy:

Imagine a master chef who, instead of following a fixed recipe, is able to adjust ingredients and cooking methods on the fly based on what's available and what the customer prefers. Metaprogramming gives your code a similar kind of adaptability.

Dynamic Method Creation with define_method

Ruby's define_method allows you to define methods dynamically within a class. This is particularly useful when you need to create many similar methods that follow a common pattern.

Example:

```ruby
class DynamicGreeter
  [:alice, :bob, :carol].each do |name|
    define_method("greet_#{name}") do
      "Hello, #{name.to_s.capitalize}!"
    end
  end
end

greeter = DynamicGreeter.new
```

```
puts greeter.greet_alice   # Outputs: Hello, Alice!
puts greeter.greet_bob     # Outputs: Hello, Bob!
```

Explanation:

This code iterates over an array of names and defines a new method for each name dynamically. The methods greet_alice, greet_bob, etc., are created at runtime.

Handling Undefined Methods with method_missing

The method_missing method is called when an object receives a message (method call) that it does not understand. Overriding method_missing can be used to create flexible interfaces that respond to a wide range of method names dynamically.

Example:

```
ruby

class DynamicResponder
  def method_missing(method, *args, &block)
    if method.to_s.start_with?("say_")
      word = method.to_s.split("say_").last
      "You asked me to say: #{word}"
    else
      super
    end
  end
```

```
  def respond_to_missing?(method, include_private =
false)
    method.to_s.start_with?("say_") || super
  end
end


responder = DynamicResponder.new
puts responder.say_hello  # Outputs: You asked me to
say: hello
```

Explanation:

Here, any method starting with say_ is intercepted by method_missing and handled dynamically.

The Power of Metaprogramming

By leveraging define_method and method_missing, you can reduce code duplication and build APIs that are both concise and flexible. This approach is particularly useful when creating DSLs, as it allows your code to adapt its behavior based on user-defined configuration.

2.2 Building Domain-Specific Languages (DSLs)

What Is a DSL?

A domain-specific language (DSL) is a mini-language tailored to a particular application domain. Unlike general-purpose programming languages, DSLs provide a syntax that is intuitive to domain experts, often resembling natural language.

Example:

Rails' routing DSL lets you define routes in a very readable manner:

```ruby

Rails.application.routes.draw do
  resources :articles
end
```

Explanation:

This DSL abstracts the underlying complexity of route definition into a few expressive lines of code.

Components of a DSL

- **Syntax:** The rules and structure that define how the DSL is written.

- **Semantics:** The meaning behind each command or statement in the DSL.

- **Parser/Interpreter:** The mechanism that reads and processes DSL commands, converting them into executable code.

Creating a DSL in Ruby

Ruby's flexible syntax and metaprogramming capabilities make it an ideal language for building DSLs. You can use blocks, instance_eval, and dynamic method definitions to create a language that is both expressive and powerful.

Example:

```ruby
ruby

class ConfigDSL
  attr_accessor :settings

  def initialize
    @settings = {}
  end

  def method_missing(name, *args, &block)
    # Treat any method call as a setting assignment
    @settings[name] = args.first || block.call
  end

  def self.build(&block)
    dsl = new
    dsl.instance_eval(&block)
    dsl.settings
  end
end

config = ConfigDSL.build do
  server "localhost"
  port 3000
  environment { "development" }
end

puts config.inspect
```

```
# Outputs: {:server=>"localhost", :port=>3000,
:environment=>"development"}
```

Explanation:

This simple DSL allows you to define configuration settings by calling methods. The method_missing intercepts calls and stores values in a hash.

2.3 Key Terminology

- **Metaprogramming:** Writing code that manipulates code at runtime.

- **define_method:** A Ruby method used to define other methods dynamically.

- **method_missing:** A Ruby hook that intercepts calls to undefined methods.

- **DSL:** A specialized mini-language designed for a particular domain.

- **instance_eval:** A method that evaluates a block of code in the context of a specific object.

2.4 Real-World Analogies

Think of metaprogramming as the art of creating flexible blueprints that adapt to the situation. If regular programming is like following a static recipe, metaprogramming is like having a smart kitchen that adjusts the recipe on the fly based on available ingredients. A DSL, then, is akin to a specialized cookbook written in a style that experts in a particular cuisine understand intuitively.

---

3. Tools and Setup

Before diving into coding, you need the proper tools and an optimized environment. This section details the setup required for exploring metaprogramming and DSLs in Ruby.

3.1 Required Tools

To work on metaprogramming and DSLs, you will need:

- **Ruby Interpreter:** Ensure Ruby is installed on your machine.

- **Version Manager (RVM or rbenv):** For managing multiple Ruby versions.

- **Text Editor or IDE:** Visual Studio Code, Sublime Text, or Atom with Ruby plugins.

- **Terminal or Command Prompt:** To run Ruby scripts and test your DSL.

- **IRB (Interactive Ruby):** For rapid prototyping of metaprogramming code.

- **Git (Optional):** For version control to track changes during experimentation.

3.2 Installing Ruby with a Version Manager

If you do not have Ruby installed, you can use RVM. Open your terminal and execute:

```bash

\curl -sSL https://get.rvm.io | bash -s stable
```
Then, install the latest Ruby:
```bash

rvm install ruby --latest
rvm use ruby --default
```
Verify installation:

```bash

ruby -v
```

3.3 Configuring Your Text Editor

For Visual Studio Code:

1. **Download and Install VS Code:** Visit code.visualstudio.com.

2. **Install Ruby Extensions:** In the Extensions view, search for "Ruby" and install an appropriate extension (e.g., Ruby by Peng Lv).

3. **Configure Settings:** Update your settings.json:

```json

```

```
{
  "editor.tabSize": 2,
  "files.trimTrailingWhitespace": true,
  "ruby.format": "rubocop"
}
```

3.4 Using IRB for Prototyping

IRB is invaluable for testing metaprogramming snippets:

- Open your terminal.

- Type irb and press Enter.

- Experiment with dynamic method creation:

```ruby
class Test
  def greet; "Hello!"; end
end

obj = Test.new
puts obj.greet  # Outputs: Hello!
```

4. Hands-on Examples & Projects

This section presents a series of practical examples that bring metaprogramming and DSL concepts to life. We start with smaller code examples demonstrating dynamic method creation, then build up to creating a mini DSL for configuration. Finally, we culminate with a project: developing a DSL for a hypothetical web service.

4.1 Example 1: Dynamic Method Creation with define_method

Exercise: Create Dynamic Greeting Methods

Create a file named dynamic_greetings.rb:

ruby

```ruby
# dynamic_greetings.rb
# This file demonstrates dynamic method creation
using define_method.

class DynamicGreeter
  [:alice, :bob, :carol].each do |name|
    define_method("greet_#{name}") do
      "Hello, #{name.to_s.capitalize}! Welcome
aboard."
    end
  end
end


greeter = DynamicGreeter.new
puts greeter.greet_alice  # => Hello, Alice! Welcome
aboard.
puts greeter.greet_bob    # => Hello, Bob! Welcome
aboard.
```

Explanation:

The class iterates over a list of names and defines methods on the fly using define_method.

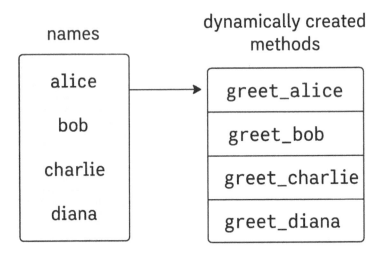

Conclusion & Next Steps

Recap of Key Points

In this chapter, we explored the powerful techniques of metaprogramming and DSL creation in Ruby. We learned how to dynamically define methods using define_method, handle undefined method calls gracefully with method_missing, and build a flexible DSL for configuration. Our hands-on project—a DSL for a hypothetical web service—demonstrated how these techniques can be combined to create an expressive and maintainable configuration language. We also discussed advanced strategies, best practices, and troubleshooting tips to ensure your metaprogramming code remains efficient and understandable.

Reflecting on the DSL Project

The web service DSL project showcased how to abstract complex configurations into a clear, declarative language. By encapsulating behavior within modules and dynamically interpreting user-defined methods, you learned how to build systems that are both powerful and intuitive. This approach not only reduces boilerplate code but also makes your application easier to extend and maintain.

Advanced Techniques and Best Practices

We covered optimization strategies such as caching dynamic method results and minimizing the reliance on method_missing when a more explicit definition is possible. Adopting these practices helps maintain performance and clarity, ensuring that your codebase remains robust as it grows in complexity.

Troubleshooting and Continued Learning

Every advanced feature introduces potential pitfalls. By using debugging tools like Pry, writing isolated tests, and following a disciplined approach to refactoring, you can overcome challenges in metaprogramming and DSL construction. Remember, continuous learning and regular code reviews are essential to mastering these advanced techniques.

Next Steps

To build upon what you've learned in this chapter:

- **Experiment Further:** Try extending the DSL project with additional configuration options, such as defining nested routes or handling more complex middleware logic.

- **Study Open-Source DSLs:** Examine popular Ruby projects that use DSLs (such as Rake or Rails routes) to see how experienced developers implement these concepts.

- **Read More:** Books like *"Metaprogramming Ruby"* provide deeper insights into Ruby's dynamic capabilities.

- **Practice:** The more you practice metaprogramming and DSL creation, the more natural it will become. Consider building small projects that incorporate these techniques.

Final Thoughts

Metaprogramming and DSLs represent some of the most powerful features Ruby has to offer. They empower you to write code that is not only flexible and reusable but also elegantly mirrors the problem domain you are addressing. By embracing these techniques, you elevate your coding from a series of repetitive tasks to an art form where your code adapts to your needs.

As you continue your journey in Ruby, remember that the power of metaprogramming comes with the responsibility to write clear, maintainable code. Always document your dynamic methods and DSL commands, and test thoroughly. With practice, these advanced techniques will become invaluable tools in your programming toolkit, enabling you to create truly expressive and efficient applications.

Chapter 9: Concurrency and Performance Tuning

---

1. Introduction

Modern applications demand responsiveness, scalability, and the ability to process multiple tasks simultaneously. Concurrency is a critical concept that addresses these needs by allowing programs to perform several operations at once. In Ruby, this topic is especially intriguing because the language has evolved significantly—from using traditional threads to introducing Ractor in Ruby 3, a powerful tool for safe parallel execution.

This chapter explores concurrency and performance tuning in Ruby. We begin by discussing concurrency fundamentals: what threads are, their limitations, and the newer Ractor abstraction that Ruby 3 offers for true parallelism. We then transition to performance topics—examining memory management, garbage collection, and practical optimization techniques that help you squeeze out every bit of performance from your code.

Why is this important? For beginners, understanding concurrency opens a door to writing applications that can handle multiple tasks simultaneously without freezing the user interface. For professionals, concurrency is essential for building scalable web services, data processing pipelines, and real-time applications. Hobbyists will appreciate the challenge and creativity required to optimize code and improve efficiency.

In this chapter, we define key concepts such as threads, race conditions, deadlocks, and the novel Ractor abstraction. We also introduce performance-related terminology like garbage collection, memory profiling, and benchmarking. Throughout, we use real-world analogies to simplify abstract concepts. For example, think of threads as workers in a factory—each capable of performing a task, but needing careful coordination to avoid chaos. Ractor, on the other hand, is like having separate factories that work in parallel without interfering with each other.

Our hands-on section guides you through a practical project: converting a multi-threaded file processor to use Ruby 3's Ractor and then profiling its performance. This project demonstrates how you can refactor legacy code to leverage modern concurrency tools, improve throughput, and optimize memory usage.

By the end of this chapter, you will understand the strengths and weaknesses of Ruby's concurrency models, know how to profile and optimize your code, and be equipped with advanced techniques for memory management and garbage collection tuning. Whether you're building a high-performance web service or a responsive desktop application, the strategies presented here will help you write efficient and robust Ruby code.

Let's dive deeper into the concepts that power Ruby's concurrency and learn how to transform your code into a finely tuned, high-performance machine.

---

2. Core Concepts and Theory

This section delves into the theoretical foundations of concurrency and performance tuning in Ruby. We will cover threads and Ractor, explain how Ruby manages memory and garbage collection, and introduce optimization techniques for high-performance code.

2.1 Concurrency Fundamentals in Ruby

Threads in Ruby

Ruby threads are units of execution that allow multiple tasks to run concurrently within a single process. Historically, Ruby's native threads have been subject to the Global Interpreter Lock (GIL), which prevents true parallel execution of Ruby code. However, threads can still be useful for I/O-bound operations, where the program waits for external resources.

Example:

```ruby
ruby

threads = []

5.times do |i|
  threads << Thread.new do
    sleep(rand(1..3))
    puts "Thread #{i} has finished."
  end
end

threads.each(&:join)
```

Explanation:

This code spawns five threads that sleep for a random time before printing a message. Although they run concurrently, the **GIL** ensures only one Ruby thread executes at a time for **CPU**-bound tasks.

Limitations of Threads

While threads can handle I/O-bound tasks efficiently, they come with challenges:

- **Race Conditions:** Multiple threads modifying shared data can lead to unpredictable results.

- **Deadlocks:** Threads waiting on each other indefinitely.

- **GIL:** Limits parallel execution in CPU-bound operations, reducing performance benefits on multi-core systems.

Introducing Ractor in Ruby 3

Ruby 3 introduces Ractor, a new abstraction for parallel execution. Ractor is designed for true parallelism by isolating execution contexts and ensuring thread safety through message passing. Each Ractor has its own object space, meaning no shared state exists, which eliminates many concurrency issues.

Example:

```ruby

ractor = Ractor.new do
  sleep 2
  "Ractor result"
end

puts "Waiting for Ractor..."
result = ractor.take
puts result  # Outputs: "Ractor result"
```

Explanation:

Here, a Ractor is created to perform a task independently. The main program continues execution and later retrieves the result using take. Unlike threads, Ractors can run in parallel on different cores.

Real-World Analogy:

Imagine threads as workers in a single office sharing a common space (and occasionally bumping into each other), whereas Ractors are like separate offices with dedicated resources, communicating only via messages.

2.2 Memory Management and Garbage Collection
Ruby's Memory Model

Ruby uses automatic memory management to allocate and free memory as needed. Objects are created dynamically, and unused objects are cleaned up by Ruby's garbage collector (GC).

Garbage Collection

Garbage collection is the process of reclaiming memory occupied by objects that are no longer in use. Ruby's GC works in several phases:

- **Mark Phase:** Identifies live objects by traversing object references.

- **Sweep Phase:** Frees memory occupied by unmarked objects.

- **Compaction (Optional):** Rearranges objects to reduce fragmentation.

Example:

ruby

```
10000.times { "string" * rand(1..10) }
GC.start  # Manually invoke garbage collection (for
demonstration only)
```

Explanation:

While manual invocation of GC is rarely needed in production, understanding its process helps in optimizing performance.

Memory Optimization Techniques

- **Object Reuse:** Avoid creating unnecessary objects; reuse existing ones when possible.

- **Lazy Evaluation:** Use lazy enumerators to delay computations until absolutely needed.

- **Profiling:** Use tools like ObjectSpace and third-party gems to monitor memory usage.

2.3 Optimization Techniques

Benchmarking Your Code

Benchmarking is essential for understanding the performance characteristics of your code. Ruby's Benchmark module provides simple methods for measuring code execution time.

Example:

```
ruby
```

```
require 'benchmark'

time = Benchmark.realtime do
  100000.times { 1 + 1 }
end
puts "Execution time: #{time} seconds"
```

Explanation:

This snippet measures how long it takes to perform a simple arithmetic operation repeatedly, allowing you to identify performance bottlenecks.

Optimizing Loops and Data Structures

Choosing the right data structures and minimizing the number of iterations can significantly improve performance. For example, prefer iterators such as each and map over manual index-based loops.

Example:

```
ruby
```

```
# Instead of using a for loop with an index:
for i in 0...array.size
  process(array[i])
end

# Use each:
array.each { |item| process(item) }
```

Explanation:

Using idiomatic Ruby iterators is not only clearer but can also offer performance improvements through internal optimizations.

2.4 Concurrency and Performance: Key Terminology

- **Thread:** A lightweight unit of execution that runs concurrently within a process.

- **Ractor:** A new concurrency abstraction in Ruby 3 for true parallel execution.

- **GIL (Global Interpreter Lock):** A mutex that prevents multiple threads from executing Ruby code simultaneously in MRI.

- **Garbage Collection (GC):** The automated process that reclaims memory from unused objects.

- **Benchmarking:** The process of measuring code performance.

- **Memory Profiling:** Tools and techniques used to analyze the memory usage of an application.

2.5 Real-World Analogies

Think of concurrency like managing a busy restaurant. Threads are like waiters who share the same kitchen (and sometimes get in each other's way), while Ractors are like separate dining rooms with dedicated chefs, ensuring that orders are processed in parallel without interference. Garbage collection is akin to a cleaning crew that regularly clears out empty tables and unwanted items, keeping the restaurant running smoothly.

---

3. Tools and Setup

Before diving into coding examples and performance profiling, you need a properly configured development environment. This section outlines the tools required and provides step-by-step instructions for setting up your Ruby environment, especially for experimenting with concurrency and Ractor.

3.1 Required Tools

To work effectively with concurrency and performance tuning in Ruby, you will need:

- **Ruby Interpreter (Ruby 3+):** To access Ractor and other modern features.

- **Version Manager (RVM or rbenv):** For managing Ruby versions.

- **Text Editor or IDE:** Visual Studio Code, Sublime Text, or Atom with Ruby plugins.

- **Terminal or Command Prompt:** To run scripts and benchmark code.

- **IRB (Interactive Ruby):** For quick experimentation.

- **Benchmark Module:** Part of Ruby's standard library for performance testing.

- **Profiling Tools:** Tools such as ObjectSpace, ruby-prof, or benchmark-ips for detailed performance analysis.

3.2 Installing Ruby with RVM

If Ruby 3 isn't installed, you can install it using RVM:

1. **Install RVM:**

bash

```
\curl -sSL https://get.rvm.io | bash -s stable
```

2. **Install Ruby 3:**

bash

```
rvm install 3.0.0
rvm use 3.0.0 --default
```

3. **Verify Installation:**

bash

```
ruby -v
```

3.3 Configuring Your Text Editor

For Visual Studio Code:

1. **Download and Install VS Code:**

   Visit code.visualstudio.com.

2. **Install Ruby Extensions:**

   Open the Extensions view (Ctrl+Shift+X) and search for "Ruby" (e.g., Ruby by Peng Lv).

3. **Configure Settings:**

   Add the following to your settings.json:

```json
{

  "editor.tabSize": 2,
  "files.trimTrailingWhitespace": true,
  "ruby.format": "rubocop"
}
```

3.4 Setting Up Benchmarking and Profiling Tools

Install profiling gems if needed:

```bash
gem install ruby-prof benchmark-ips
```

3.5 Using IRB for Experimentation

IRB is a quick way to test concurrency code:

- Launch IRB:

```bash
irb
```

- Experiment with threads and Ractor:

```ruby
Thread.new { sleep 1; "Thread finished" }
r = Ractor.new { sleep 1; "Ractor finished" }
puts r.take
```

4. Hands-on Examples & Projects

This section offers a series of practical examples and a comprehensive project that applies the concepts of concurrency and performance tuning. We start with simple examples of using threads and Ractor, then gradually move towards converting an existing multi-threaded file processor to use Ractor, and finally profile its performance.

4.1 Example 1: Basic Thread Usage
Exercise: Create a Multi-threaded Greeting

Create a file named thread_greetings.rb:

```ruby
```

```ruby
# thread_greetings.rb
# This script demonstrates creating and joining
threads.

threads = []

5.times do |i|
  threads << Thread.new do
    sleep(rand(0.5..2))
    puts "Thread #{i} says hello!"
  end
end

threads.each(&:join)
puts "All threads have finished."
```

Explanation:

This code creates five threads that sleep for a random duration before printing a message. The threads are then joined, ensuring the main program waits for them to complete.

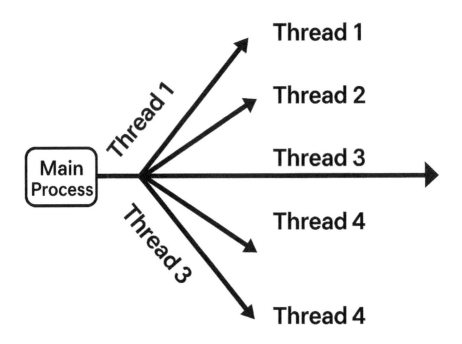

4.2 Example 2: Introducing Ractor

Exercise: Simple Ractor Example

Create a file named ractor_greetings.rb:

ruby

```
# ractor_greetings.rb
# Demonstrates the use of Ractor for parallel
execution.
```

```
ractor = Ractor.new do
   sleep 1
   "Ractor says hello!"
end

puts "Waiting for Ractor..."
result = ractor.take
puts result
```

Explanation:

This code creates a Ractor that sleeps for a second and then returns a message. The main program continues and then retrieves the result, illustrating parallel execution without shared state.

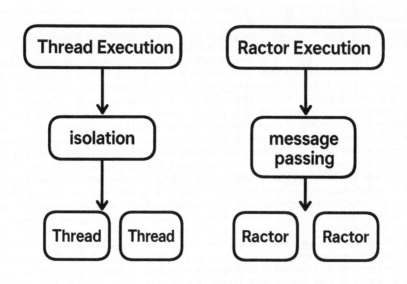

Conclusion & Next Steps

Recap of Key Points

In this chapter, we explored the critical topics of concurrency and performance tuning in Ruby. We began by discussing traditional threads, their limitations under the GIL, and how Ruby 3's Ractor provides true parallelism. We then examined memory management, garbage collection, and optimization techniques such as benchmarking and profiling. Our hands-on project demonstrated how to convert a multi-threaded file processor to use Ractor and profile its performance, illustrating the practical benefits of these techniques.

Reflecting on the Project

The project showcased how modern concurrency features in Ruby can improve the performance of I/O and CPU-bound operations. By refactoring a legacy file processor, you learned to leverage Ractor's isolation for safe parallelism and to measure performance improvements using Ruby's benchmarking tools. This practical exercise underscores the importance of staying current with language advancements to build scalable applications.

Advanced Techniques and Best Practices

We discussed advanced strategies for minimizing concurrency overhead, optimizing memory usage, and profiling code. Adopting these best practices—such as using mutexes for thread safety, caching expensive computations, and benchmarking hot code paths—ensures that your applications not only perform well but also remain maintainable over time.

Troubleshooting and Continued Learning

Debugging concurrent applications can be challenging, but tools like Pry, ruby-prof, and Benchmark-IPS, along with careful logging and systematic troubleshooting, make the process manageable. Continuous learning, code reviews, and performance monitoring are essential practices as your applications scale.

Next Steps

As you move forward:

- **Experiment Further:** Enhance your file processor project with additional features such as error handling, dynamic workload balancing, and more complex data processing.

- **Explore Other Concurrency Models:** Investigate libraries and frameworks that provide additional concurrency abstractions.

- **Invest in Performance Profiling:** Regularly profile your applications to catch performance regressions early.

- **Engage with the Community:** Participate in Ruby conferences and forums to share experiences and learn from other developers.

Final Thoughts

Concurrency and performance tuning are advanced topics that can significantly elevate the quality and responsiveness of your applications. Ruby's evolution—from traditional threads to Ractor—demonstrates the language's commitment to modern, scalable development practices. By mastering these techniques, you not only improve the performance of your applications but also gain the ability to write robust, concurrent code that stands up to real-world demands.

Remember, the journey to performance optimization is continuous. Keep profiling, refactoring, and learning as new tools and techniques emerge. With persistence and a systematic approach, you can build Ruby applications that are both fast and reliable.

Chapter 10: Building Command-Line and Automation Tools

1. Introduction

In today's fast-paced digital world, command-line interfaces (CLIs) and automation tools are indispensable for developers, system administrators, and hobbyists alike. They allow you to interact directly with your computer's operating system, automate repetitive tasks, and process data in ways that graphical user interfaces (GUIs) often cannot match in flexibility and efficiency.

This chapter focuses on how to build command-line applications and automation scripts using Ruby. We begin by discussing the importance of CLI tools and automation—explaining how they can drastically improve productivity and streamline processes. You'll learn the key concepts and terminology behind CLI development, such as argument parsing, standard input/output, and exit codes. We'll also introduce core ideas of automation, including file manipulation, batch processing, and scheduling periodic tasks.

For beginners, this chapter lays out the fundamentals of creating simple yet powerful command-line tools. For professionals, it offers advanced techniques to build scalable and robust automation scripts. And for hobbyists, it opens the door to creatively solving everyday problems by writing scripts that perform complex tasks with just a few commands.

Imagine a scenario where you need to manage a long to-do list, update a series of configuration files, or schedule regular system maintenance. A well-designed CLI tool or automation script not only saves time but also reduces errors by eliminating manual intervention. Throughout this chapter, we'll use real-world analogies—comparing a CLI to a toolbox that gives you quick access to powerful functions, or automation to a personal assistant that handles repetitive chores—to illustrate these ideas.

In our hands-on project, you will build a task manager CLI that lets users add, view, update, and remove tasks, along with a scheduler that triggers periodic task reminders. This project will combine command-line argument parsing, file input/output (I/O) for data persistence, and scheduling logic to demonstrate how these concepts work together in a cohesive application.

By the end of this chapter, you'll not only have a solid understanding of building CLIs and automation tools in Ruby but also practical experience in writing clean, well-documented, and maintainable code. Whether you plan to integrate these skills into your professional workflow or use them to solve everyday challenges, you're about to discover a world of possibilities that empowers you to take control of your computing environment.

---

2. Core Concepts and Theory

In this section, we delve deeply into the theoretical foundations behind building CLI applications and automation tools. We break the discussion into key concepts, covering both command-line interfaces and automation techniques. Our focus is on clarity, practical examples, and real-world analogies.

2.1 Understanding Command-Line Interfaces (CLIs)
What Is a CLI?

A command-line interface is a text-based user interface used to interact with software or the operating system. Unlike graphical interfaces, CLIs rely solely on typed commands. They offer unmatched speed, flexibility, and automation capabilities.

- **Key Components of a CLI:**
  - **Arguments and Options:** Users pass parameters to the command, specifying what action to perform.

- o **Standard Input/Output (STDIN/STDOUT):** CLIs read input from the user (or piped input) and display output in the terminal.

- o **Exit Codes:** Commands return exit statuses to indicate success or failure.

Analogy:

Imagine a **CLI** as a remote control for your TV—every button (command) has a specific function, and by pressing different buttons (passing arguments), you change the channel, adjust volume, or access special features.

Parsing Command-Line Arguments

To build effective **CLI** tools, you need to parse user input. Ruby provides libraries like OptionParser to simplify this task.

Example:

```ruby
require 'optparse'

options = {}
OptionParser.new do |opts|
  opts.banner = "Usage: task_manager.rb [options]"
```

```ruby
opts.on("-a", "--add TASK", "Add a new task") do
|task|
    options[:add] = task
  end


  opts.on("-l", "--list", "List all tasks") do
    options[:list] = true
  end


  opts.on("-r", "--remove INDEX", "Remove a task by
index") do |index|
    options[:remove] = index.to_i
  end
end.parse!


puts options.inspect
```

Explanation:

This snippet uses OptionParser to define a simple interface that accepts options to add, list, or remove tasks. Each option is stored in a hash for further processing.

2.2 Automation Through Scripting

What Is Automation?

Automation refers to the creation of scripts or tools that perform repetitive tasks automatically. In Ruby, automation can involve file manipulation, data processing, system administration tasks, and more.

- **File Manipulation:** Reading, writing, and modifying files.

- **Batch Processing:** Running operations on multiple files or data sets.

- **Scheduling Tasks:** Executing scripts periodically using built-in schedulers or external tools like cron.

Analogy:

Think of automation as a personal assistant who takes care of routine tasks such as organizing your desk, scheduling appointments, and sending reminders—freeing you to focus on more important matters.

File I/O in Ruby

Ruby's standard library makes file manipulation straightforward.

Example:

```ruby
ruby

# Reading a file
content = File.read("tasks.txt")
puts content

# Writing to a file
File.open("tasks.txt", "w") do |file|
  file.puts "Task 1: Buy groceries"
  file.puts "Task 2: Complete assignment"
```

```
end
```

Explanation:

This code shows how to read the entire content of a file and write new content to a file using Ruby's File class.

Scheduling Tasks

For periodic tasks, you can use Ruby's built-in scheduler libraries or external tools.

Example using the 'rufus-scheduler' gem:

```ruby
ruby

require 'rufus-scheduler'

scheduler = Rufus::Scheduler.new

scheduler.every '10s' do
  puts "This message is printed every 10 seconds."
end

scheduler.join
```

Explanation:

The above code sets up a scheduler that executes a block every 10 seconds. This is useful for tasks like sending reminders or updating logs.

2.3 Key Terminology

- **CLI (Command-Line Interface):** A text-based interface for interacting with programs.

- **OptionParser:** A Ruby library for parsing command-line options.

- **STDIN/STDOUT:** Standard input/output streams used for reading user input and displaying output.

- **Automation:** The process of making a system perform tasks automatically.

- **File I/O:** Operations for reading from and writing to files.

- **Scheduler:** A tool or library used to run tasks periodically.

2.4 Real-World Analogies

Visualize a CLI as your car's dashboard—each button and gauge provides essential information and control. Automation is like having a programmable thermostat at home: it adjusts the temperature based on pre-set rules without you having to intervene constantly. Together, these tools transform manual, repetitive tasks into seamless, efficient processes.

3. Tools and Setup

Before building your CLI and automation tools, ensure your development environment is ready. This section walks you through the required tools and provides step-by-step instructions for setting up your Ruby environment.

3.1 Required Tools

To create robust CLI applications and automation scripts, you will need:

- **Ruby Interpreter (preferably Ruby 3+):** To run your Ruby code.

- **Version Manager (RVM or rbenv):** To manage Ruby versions.

- **Text Editor or IDE:** Visual Studio Code, Sublime Text, or Atom with Ruby plugins.

- **Terminal or Command Prompt:** To execute your scripts.

- **Gems:**

    o **OptionParser:** Part of Ruby's standard library for CLI argument parsing.

    o **Rufus-Scheduler:** For scheduling periodic tasks.

    o **Bundler:** For managing gem dependencies.

3.2 Installing Ruby with RVM

If Ruby is not installed, use RVM to install it:

1. **Install RVM:**

```bash
```

```bash
\curl -sSL https://get.rvm.io | bash -s stable
```

2. **Install the Latest Ruby Version:**

```bash
```

```bash
rvm install ruby --latest
rvm use ruby --default
```

3. **Verify Installation:**

```bash
```

```bash
ruby -v
```

3.3 Configuring Your Text Editor

For Visual Studio Code:

1. **Download and Install VS Code:**
   Visit code.visualstudio.com to download.

2. **Install Ruby Extensions:**
   Open the Extensions view (Ctrl+Shift+X or Cmd+Shift+X)
   and install a Ruby extension (e.g., Ruby by Peng Lv).

3. **Configure Settings:**

Update your settings.json:

```json
{
  "editor.tabSize": 2,
  "files.trimTrailingWhitespace": true,
  "ruby.format": "rubocop"
}
```

3.4 Installing Required Gems

Use Bundler to manage dependencies. Create a Gemfile in your project directory:

```ruby
source "https://rubygems.org"

gem 'rufus-scheduler'
```

Then install the gems:

```bash
bundle install
```

3.5 Using IRB for Quick Testing

IRB (Interactive Ruby) is invaluable for quickly testing small code snippets:

- Open your terminal.

- Type:

```bash
irb
```

Test a simple file I/O operation:

```ruby
File.write("test.txt", "Hello, Ruby!")
puts File.read("test.txt")
```

---

4. Hands-on Examples & Projects

In this section, we present practical examples and a comprehensive project that combines CLI tool building with automation. We begin with smaller examples and then work on a full-fledged task manager CLI and scheduler.

4.1 Example 1: Building a Simple CLI
Exercise: A Basic Task Manager CLI

Create a file named task_manager.rb:

```ruby
#!/usr/bin/env ruby
# task_manager.rb
```

```ruby
# A simple CLI task manager that lets users add and
list tasks.

require 'optparse'

# Data store for tasks (in-memory for simplicity)
$tasks = []

options = {}
OptionParser.new do |opts|
  opts.banner = "Usage: task_manager.rb [options]"

  opts.on("-aTASK", "--add=TASK", "Add a new task")
do |task|
    options[:add] = task
  end

  opts.on("-l", "--list", "List all tasks") do
    options[:list] = true
  end
end.parse!

if options[:add]
  $tasks << options[:add]
  puts "Task added: #{options[:add]}"
elsif options[:list]
  if $tasks.empty?
    puts "No tasks available."
  else
```

```
    puts "Tasks:"
    $tasks.each_with_index { |task, index| puts
"#{index + 1}. #{task}" }
  end
else
  puts "Please provide an option. Use -h for help."
end
```

Explanation:

This script uses OptionParser to handle command-line arguments for adding and listing tasks. Tasks are stored in a global array for demonstration purposes.

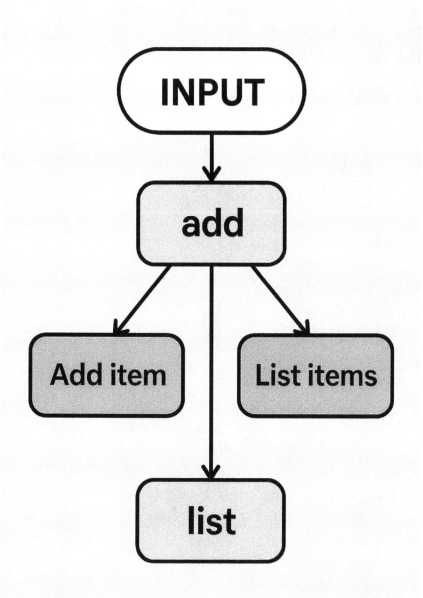

4.2 Example 2: Automation with File Manipulation

Exercise: Automating Log File Cleanup

Create a file named log_cleaner.rb:

ruby

```ruby
#!/usr/bin/env ruby
# log_cleaner.rb
# A simple script to archive log files older than a
specified number of days.

require 'fileutils'
require 'date'

LOG_DIR = "./logs"
ARCHIVE_DIR = "./archive"
DAYS_THRESHOLD = 7

Dir.mkdir(ARCHIVE_DIR) unless Dir.exist?(ARCHIVE_DIR)

Dir.glob("#{LOG_DIR}/*.log") do |file|
  if File.mtime(file) < (Date.today -
DAYS_THRESHOLD).to_time
    FileUtils.mv(file, ARCHIVE_DIR)
    puts "Archived #{file}"
  end
end
```

```
puts "Log cleanup complete."
```

Explanation:

This script automates the archiving of log files that are older than seven days. It demonstrates file manipulation, directory creation, and date comparison.

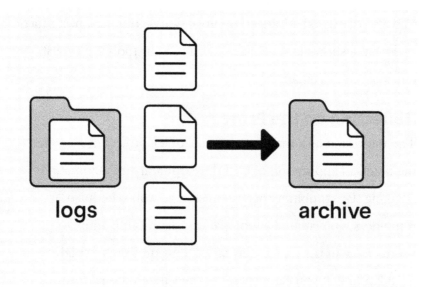

logs   archive

Conclusion & Next Steps

Recap of Key Points

In this chapter, we explored how to build command-line and automation tools using Ruby. We started with the fundamentals of creating CLIs—parsing command-line arguments, reading from STDIN, and providing user feedback. We then moved into automation, covering file manipulation, batch processing, and task scheduling using tools like Rufus-Scheduler.

Through a series of hands-on examples, you learned how to build a simple task manager CLI, enhance it with persistent storage, and integrate a scheduler to periodically remind you of pending tasks. We also discussed advanced optimization techniques, best practices, and troubleshooting strategies to ensure your tools are robust, efficient, and maintainable.

Reflecting on the Project

The integrated task manager and scheduler project demonstrated the practical application of CLI development and automation scripting. By combining persistent storage with scheduled reminders, you created a tool that can significantly improve productivity in managing daily tasks. This project is a solid foundation that you can expand upon with additional features such as categorization, task prioritization, and integration with external APIs.

Troubleshooting and Continued Learning

As with any software project, challenges will arise. The troubleshooting strategies discussed—using logging, dry runs, and step-by-step testing—are critical for identifying and resolving issues in your CLI and automation tools. Remember that continuous learning and iterative improvement are key to building robust applications.

Next Steps

To further develop your skills in building CLI and automation tools:

- **Expand Your Projects:** Enhance the task manager with features like notifications, multi-user support, or integration with calendar APIs.

- **Explore More Gems:** Investigate additional Ruby gems that facilitate automation, such as Thor for CLI building or Sidekiq for background processing.

- **Participate in Open Source:** Contribute to existing CLI projects or create your own open-source tool to receive feedback and improve your skills.

- **Stay Updated:** Follow Ruby community blogs, forums, and conferences to learn about emerging trends and best practices in automation and CLI development.

Final Thoughts

Building command-line and automation tools is a powerful way to streamline your workflow and solve everyday problems efficiently. The skills you've gained in this chapter—from parsing command-line arguments to scheduling periodic tasks—are essential for any developer looking to enhance productivity and create maintainable, scalable systems. As you continue to experiment and refine your code, you will discover that these tools not only save time but also empower you to tackle more complex challenges with confidence.

Remember that the journey to mastering automation is ongoing. Embrace iterative improvement, learn from each project, and share your insights with the community. With persistence and creativity, you can build tools that make a real difference in your daily work and beyond.

Chapter 11: Web Development and RESTful APIs

1. Introduction

Modern web development is evolving rapidly, and Ruby remains at the forefront thanks to its elegant frameworks and developer-friendly syntax. In this chapter, we explore the world of web development and RESTful APIs using Ruby. Whether you're a beginner learning the ropes, a professional aiming to build scalable applications, or a hobbyist excited about new projects, this chapter provides the knowledge and practical examples needed to create both web applications and RESTful services.

At its core, web development involves building applications that interact with users via browsers or other clients. Ruby's frameworks—Sinatra and Ruby on Rails—offer powerful tools to build dynamic, maintainable web apps quickly. Sinatra is a lightweight framework ideal for simple applications and APIs, while Ruby on Rails provides a comprehensive structure for building full-featured applications following the Model-View-Controller (MVC) pattern.

RESTful APIs are the backbone of modern web services. They allow different systems to communicate over HTTP, providing a standardized way to access resources. Understanding how to design, implement, and test RESTful APIs is crucial for building web services that are both robust and scalable. In this chapter, we cover the basics of REST principles, such as resource-based URIs, HTTP verbs (GET, POST, PUT, DELETE), status codes, and JSON responses.

We begin by discussing the significance of web frameworks and RESTful APIs, along with key terminology. Next, we dive into the core concepts and theory behind building web applications with Sinatra and Rails, using real-world analogies to simplify complex ideas. Then, we walk you through the tools and setup required for a modern Ruby web development environment. Finally, you'll work on a comprehensive hands-on project: developing a to-do API complete with testing instructions. This project integrates web app development and API design, showing you how to create an application that can be easily extended and maintained.

Imagine building a to-do list application where users can manage their daily tasks via a RESTful interface. Not only does this demonstrate CRUD (Create, Read, Update, Delete) operations, but it also teaches you how to expose your application's functionality to other systems. Whether you plan to build a blog, a task manager, or any web-based application, mastering these concepts will empower you to design applications that are easy to understand, extend, and scale.

Throughout this chapter, we will provide clean, well-commented code examples. We'll include diagrams to illustrate the flow of data in a RESTful API, screenshots of development environments, and visual aids to help conceptualize MVC architecture and HTTP request handling. By the end of this chapter, you'll be well-equipped to build both web applications and robust APIs using Ruby's powerful frameworks.

Let's embark on this journey to learn how to build web applications and RESTful APIs that are not only functional but also clean, maintainable, and scalable.

2. Core Concepts and Theory

In this section, we explore the theoretical underpinnings of web development and RESTful API design in Ruby. We cover key concepts such as web frameworks, MVC architecture, HTTP methods, and REST principles, using clear explanations, analogies, and real-world examples.

2.1 Web Frameworks: Sinatra and Ruby on Rails

Sinatra

Sinatra is a lightweight web framework in Ruby designed for simplicity and minimalism. It allows you to quickly create web applications with a few lines of code. Sinatra is ideal for building small web apps, APIs, or prototypes.

Key Features:

- Minimal boilerplate: Write less code to get started.

- Flexibility: Easily extend and customize your application.

- Simplicity: Ideal for simple applications and microservices.

Example:

```ruby
require 'sinatra'

get '/' do
  "Welcome to my Sinatra app!"
end
```

Explanation:

This code snippet creates a simple web server that responds with a welcome message when the root URL is accessed.

Ruby on Rails

Ruby on Rails (RoR) is a full-stack web application framework that follows the MVC (Model-View-Controller) pattern. Rails provides a structured environment and many built-in features such as ORM (ActiveRecord), routing, and automated testing. It is designed to encourage convention over configuration.

Key Features:

- MVC Architecture: Separates concerns into models, views, and controllers.

- Convention Over Configuration: Minimizes the need for extensive configuration.

- Rich Ecosystem: Provides tools for testing, database migrations, and more.

Example:

```ruby
```

```ruby
# In Rails, routes are defined in config/routes.rb
Rails.application.routes.draw do
  root "welcome#index"
end
```

Explanation:

This snippet defines the root route of a Rails application, directing requests to the index action of a Welcome controller.

2.2 RESTful API Fundamentals

REST (Representational State Transfer) is an architectural style that defines a set of constraints for creating web services. A RESTful API uses standard HTTP methods and status codes to interact with resources.

Key Concepts:

- **Resources:** The objects or data (e.g., tasks, users) that the API exposes.

- **HTTP Methods:**

  o GET: Retrieve a resource.

  o POST: Create a new resource.

  o PUT/PATCH: Update an existing resource.

  o DELETE: Remove a resource.

- **Status Codes:** Indicate the result of the HTTP request (e.g., 200 OK, 404 Not Found).

- **Statelessness:** Each API request contains all the information needed to process it.

Real-World Analogy:

Think of a RESTful API as a waiter at a restaurant. You (the client) place an order (HTTP request) for a specific dish (resource) using the menu (URI). The waiter processes your order and brings back the dish (response), along with a status indicating success or failure.

2.3 MVC Architecture in Web Development

MVC (Model-View-Controller) is a design pattern that separates an application into three interconnected components:

- **Model:** Handles data and business logic.

- **View:** Manages the presentation layer.

- **Controller:** Processes incoming requests, interacts with the model, and selects the appropriate view.

Example in Rails:

- **Model:** A Post class that represents blog posts.

- **View:** HTML templates that display blog content.

- **Controller:** A PostsController that handles requests to create, update, or display posts.

Analogy:

Imagine a newspaper:

- **Model:** The reporters who gather and verify the news (data and logic).

- **View:** The printed newspaper layout (presentation).

- **Controller:** The editor who decides which stories to publish and how to organize them.

2.4 API Design and Testing Principles

When designing a RESTful API, consider the following:

- **Resource Naming:** Use plural nouns for resources (e.g., /tasks, /users).

- **Versioning:** Plan for API evolution by versioning endpoints (e.g., /v1/tasks).

- **Documentation:** Provide clear API documentation for users.

- **Testing:** Automate testing with tools like RSpec to ensure your API behaves as expected.

Example Test with RSpec:

```ruby
require 'rspec'
require 'net/http'
require 'json'

RSpec.describe "To-Do API" do
  it "returns a list of tasks" do
    uri = URI("http://localhost:4567/tasks")
    response = Net::HTTP.get(uri)
    tasks = JSON.parse(response)
```

```
    expect(tasks).to be_an_instance_of(Array)
  end
end
```

Explanation:

This test sends an HTTP GET request to the /tasks endpoint and checks that the response is an array of tasks.

2.5 Key Terminology

- **Web Framework:** A software framework that simplifies web application development.

- **MVC:** A design pattern that separates concerns into models, views, and controllers.

- **REST:** An architectural style for building scalable web services.

- **CRUD:** An acronym for Create, Read, Update, Delete— basic operations for resource management.

- **Endpoint:** A URL where an API can be accessed.

2.6 Real-World Analogies

Consider a web application like a busy library:

- **Models (Books, Users):** Represent the library's resources.

- **Views (Catalogs, Web Pages):** Display the library's contents.

- **Controllers (Librarians):** Manage requests, helping users find and check out books.

- **RESTful API:** Functions like an automated catalog system where you can request information about a book or update your user profile via simple HTTP commands.

---

3. Tools and Setup

Before building web applications and APIs with Ruby, you need a well-equipped development environment. This section covers the tools required and provides step-by-step instructions for setting up your system.

3.1 Required Tools

To work on web development and RESTful APIs in Ruby, you will need:

- **Ruby Interpreter (preferably Ruby 3+):** To run your web application code.

- **Version Manager (RVM or rbenv):** For managing Ruby versions.

- **Text Editor or IDE:** Visual Studio Code, Sublime Text, or Atom with Ruby plugins.

- **Terminal or Command Prompt:** To execute commands and run servers.

- **Sinatra and Rails Gems:** For building web applications.

- **Bundler:** For managing gem dependencies.

- **Testing Frameworks:** RSpec or Minitest for API testing.

- **HTTP Client Tools:** Tools like cURL or Postman for testing endpoints.

3.2 Installing Ruby with a Version Manager

If Ruby is not installed, use RVM:

1. **Install RVM:**

```bash
```

```bash
\curl -sSL https://get.rvm.io | bash -s stable
```

2. **Install Ruby 3+:**

```bash
```

```bash
rvm install ruby --latest
rvm use ruby --default
```

3. **Verify Installation:**

```bash
```

```bash
ruby -v
```

3.3 Setting Up Your Framework

Sinatra Setup

1. **Create a Project Directory:**

bash

```bash
mkdir my_sinatra_app && cd my_sinatra_app
```

2. **Initialize Bundler:**

bash

```bash
bundle init
```

3. **Add Sinatra to Your Gemfile:**

ruby

```ruby
# Gemfile
gem 'sinatra'
```

4. **Install Gems:**

bash

```bash
bundle install
```

5. **Create a Basic Sinatra App:**

ruby

```ruby
# app.rb
require 'sinatra'
```

```
get '/' do
  "Welcome to Sinatra!"
end
```

6. **Run the App:**

```
bash
```

```
ruby app.rb
```

Visual Aid:

A screenshot of a browser displaying "Welcome to Sinatra!"

Ruby on Rails Setup

1. **Install Rails:**

```
bash
```

```
gem install rails
```

2. **Create a New Rails App:**

```
bash
```

```
rails new my_rails_app
cd my_rails_app
```

3. **Start the Server:**

```
bash
```

```
rails server
```

3.4 Installing Testing and API Tools

1. **RSpec Setup (for Sinatra or Rails):**

    o   Add to your Gemfile:

```ruby
group :test do
  gem 'rspec'
end
```

    o   Run:

```bash
bundle install
rspec --init
```

2. **HTTP Client Tools:**

    o   Use cURL or Postman to send test requests to your
        API endpoints.

---

4. Hands-on Examples & Projects

This section provides practical examples and a comprehensive
project that illustrates building a web application and a RESTful
API. We begin with small, focused examples and then work our way
up to a complete project.

4.1 Example 1: A Simple Blog Application Using Sinatra

Exercise: Create a Basic CRUD Blog with Sinatra

Create a file named blog_app.rb:

ruby

```ruby
# blog_app.rb
require 'sinatra'
require 'json'

# In-memory store for posts
$posts = []

# List all posts
get '/posts' do
  content_type :json
  $posts.to_json
end

# Create a new post
post '/posts' do
  data = JSON.parse(request.body.read)
  $posts << { id: $posts.size + 1, title:
data["title"], content: data["content"] }
  status 201
end

# Retrieve a specific post
```

```ruby
get '/posts/:id' do
  content_type :json
  post = $posts.find { |p| p[:id] == params[:id].to_i
}
  if post
    post.to_json
  else
    status 404
  end
end

# Update a post
put '/posts/:id' do
  data = JSON.parse(request.body.read)
  post = $posts.find { |p| p[:id] == params[:id].to_i
}
  if post
    post[:title] = data["title"]
    post[:content] = data["content"]
    status 200
  else
    status 404
  end
end

# Delete a post
delete '/posts/:id' do
  post = $posts.find { |p| p[:id] == params[:id].to_i
}
```

```
  if post
    $posts.delete(post)
    status 200
  else
    status 404
  end
end
```

Explanation:

This Sinatra app demonstrates basic CRUD operations for a blog. Posts are stored in an in-memory array and served as JSON responses.

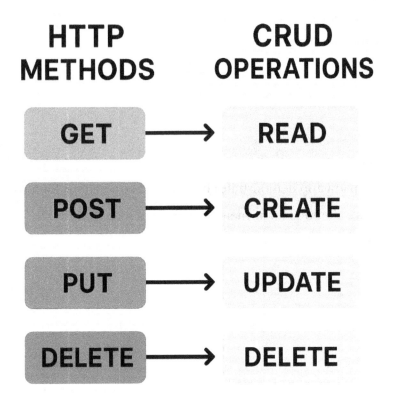

4.2 Example 2: RESTful API Testing with RSpec

Exercise: Write Tests for the Blog API

Create a file named spec/blog_api_spec.rb:

ruby

```ruby
# spec/blog_api_spec.rb
require 'rspec'
require 'rack/test'
```

```ruby
require_relative '../blog_app'

RSpec.describe 'Blog API' do
  include Rack::Test::Methods

  def app
    Sinatra::Application
  end

  it "creates a new post" do
    post '/posts', { title: "First Post", content:
"Hello World" }.to_json, "CONTENT_TYPE" =>
"application/json"
    expect(last_response.status).to eq(201)
  end

  it "lists all posts" do
    get '/posts'
    expect(last_response).to be_ok
    posts = JSON.parse(last_response.body)
    expect(posts).to be_an_instance_of(Array)
  end
end
```

Explanation:

This RSpec test uses Rack::Test to simulate HTTP requests to the Sinatra app and verifies that the endpoints work as expected.

Conclusion & Next Steps

Recap of Key Points

In this chapter, we explored the fundamentals of web development and RESTful API design using Ruby. We discussed the role of web frameworks—comparing the simplicity of Sinatra with the full-stack power of Ruby on Rails—and examined the principles of RESTful API design. We then provided detailed, practical examples of building a simple blog or CRUD application and guiding you through the design, development, and testing of a to-do API.

Reflecting on the Project

Our comprehensive to-do API project illustrated how to create a RESTful service from scratch, including:

- Handling HTTP requests and responses.

- Implementing CRUD operations.

- Writing comprehensive tests to ensure API reliability.

- Providing meaningful error messages and status codes.

This project not only reinforced RESTful principles but also demonstrated best practices for designing APIs that are scalable and maintainable.

Advanced Techniques and Optimization

We covered advanced techniques such as caching, load testing, API versioning, and security best practices. These strategies ensure that your web applications and APIs perform well under real-world conditions and are robust enough to evolve with changing requirements.

Troubleshooting and Continued Learning

Every web application faces challenges—from routing errors to JSON parsing issues. The troubleshooting strategies discussed in this chapter, such as detailed logging, interactive debugging, and isolated testing, will help you identify and resolve issues efficiently. Embrace these practices to continuously improve your development workflow.

Next Steps

As you continue your journey in web development:

- **Expand Your Projects:** Consider integrating a database for persistent storage, adding authentication, or building additional endpoints.

- **Explore More Frameworks:** Delve deeper into Ruby on Rails or experiment with lightweight alternatives like Sinatra for microservices.

- **Invest in Testing:** Adopt a comprehensive testing strategy using CI/CD pipelines.

- **Engage with the Community:** Participate in open-source projects, attend Ruby meetups, and share your experiences with fellow developers.

- **Stay Current:** Follow blogs, forums, and conferences to keep up with the latest trends in web development and API design.

Final Thoughts

Web development and RESTful APIs are powerful tools that allow you to create applications that communicate effectively over the web. By mastering these techniques, you not only build functional applications but also create scalable, maintainable, and robust systems that can evolve over time. The skills you have acquired in this chapter—from understanding web frameworks and MVC architecture to designing and testing RESTful APIs—are fundamental to modern software development.

Remember that building high-quality web applications is a continuous process of learning, testing, and refining. With persistence, attention to detail, and a commitment to best practices, you can create systems that are both elegant and effective. Embrace the challenge, keep experimenting, and let your creativity drive you to develop applications that truly stand out.

Chapter 12: Modern Trends and Community Engagement

1. Introduction

The Ruby programming language has always been known for its elegant syntax and developer-friendly design. In recent years, Ruby has continued to evolve with modern enhancements and trends that not only improve the language's performance and expressiveness but also empower developers to write more secure, maintainable, and high-quality code. This chapter explores the modern trends shaping Ruby's future, including new features in Ruby 3 such as pattern matching and Ractor, as well as best practices for security, static analysis, and overall code quality.

Modern Ruby development goes beyond simply writing code that "works." Developers are increasingly expected to produce software that is secure, efficient, and easy to maintain. This chapter is particularly relevant for beginners who want to learn best practices from the start, professionals looking to refine their workflows with the latest tools and techniques, and hobbyists who enjoy building projects that adhere to industry standards.

We start by introducing key new features in Ruby 3, such as pattern matching—a powerful tool for deconstructing complex data structures—and Ractor, which provides true parallelism by allowing safe, concurrent execution. These enhancements not only boost performance but also open up new design possibilities for building scalable applications.

Next, we delve into best practices for ensuring that your code is secure and maintainable. We discuss static analysis tools, such as RuboCop and Brakeman, that help enforce coding standards and detect vulnerabilities early in the development process. We also cover tips for writing secure code, such as proper input sanitization, the use of secure libraries, and techniques for minimizing potential attack vectors.

Beyond code quality, real-world applications of Ruby can be found in industries ranging from manufacturing and healthcare to logistics and finance. Case studies from these fields illustrate how Ruby's flexibility and ease of use translate into practical solutions for complex, data-driven problems. We explore examples of Ruby applications that have been deployed in these sectors, highlighting the lessons learned and best practices adopted by experienced developers.

Finally, the strength of Ruby lies in its vibrant community. Engaging with the community is crucial for staying updated with the latest trends, receiving support, and contributing to the language's evolution. We discuss how to contribute to open source projects, join local or online user groups, and leverage community resources to continue your learning journey. Whether you're looking to share your expertise or learn from others, community engagement is a key part of becoming a proficient Ruby developer.

This chapter sets the tone for a deep dive into modern Ruby practices. It provides a roadmap for harnessing the latest language features, adopting industry best practices for security and code quality, and actively participating in the Ruby community. As you read on, you'll discover that staying current with modern trends is not only about improving your own skill set—it's about contributing to and growing with a dynamic community of like-minded developers.

2. Core Concepts and Theory

In this section, we explore the core concepts underlying modern Ruby trends and community engagement. We begin by examining Ruby 3's latest features, then move into best practices for security and code quality, and finally discuss real-world applications and community engagement.

2.1 Ruby 3 Enhancements
Pattern Matching

Pattern matching is one of the most anticipated features in Ruby 3. It allows you to match complex data structures against patterns in a concise and readable way. Pattern matching in Ruby is similar to switch-case statements found in other languages but offers a much richer syntax.

Example:

ruby

```
def classify(value)
  case value
  in Integer
    "This is an integer."
  in String
    "This is a string."
  in [Integer, Integer]
    "This is an array with two integers."
  else
    "Unknown type."
  end
end

puts classify(42)                # => "This is an
integer."
```

```
puts classify("hello")          # => "This is a
string."
puts classify([1, 2])           # => "This is an array
with two integers."
puts classify([1, "two"])       # => "Unknown type."
```

Explanation:

Here, the in clauses allow the method to "pattern match" the value against various conditions. Pattern matching makes code more expressive and reduces the need for nested conditionals.

Ractor

Ruby 3's Ractor introduces true parallelism by providing isolated execution contexts that safely run concurrently. Unlike traditional threads, Ractors do not share mutable state, which greatly reduces the risk of race conditions.

Example:

```ruby
ractor = Ractor.new do
  sleep 1
  "Result from Ractor"
end

puts "Waiting for Ractor..."
result = ractor.take
puts result  # Outputs: "Result from Ractor"
```

Explanation:

This simple example demonstrates creating a Ractor that executes code independently. The main program continues its execution and then retrieves the result with take. Ractors are especially beneficial for CPU-bound tasks on multi-core machines.

2.2 Best Practices for Security and Code Quality
Static Analysis and Code Quality

Tools like RuboCop, Brakeman, and Reek help enforce coding standards, detect vulnerabilities, and identify code smells. These tools automatically analyze your code and provide feedback on issues that could affect security or maintainability.

Example RuboCop Configuration:

```yaml
AllCops:
  TargetRubyVersion: 3.0
  Exclude:
    - 'db/schema.rb'

Layout/LineLength:
  Max: 100

Style/StringLiterals:
  EnforcedStyle: double_quotes
```

Explanation:

A configuration file like the one above tells RuboCop what standards to enforce, ensuring your code remains clean and consistent.

Security Best Practices

When writing Ruby code, especially for web applications and APIs, security is paramount. Here are a few best practices:

- **Input Validation and Sanitization:** Ensure that all external inputs are validated and sanitized to prevent injection attacks.

- **Use Secure Libraries:** Prefer libraries that are actively maintained and have strong security records.

- **Minimal Privilege:** Run your applications with the least privileges necessary.

- **Regular Updates:** Keep Ruby and its gems up-to-date to patch known vulnerabilities.

Real-World Analogy:

Consider these practices like locking your doors and windows at home. Just as you wouldn't leave your house unprotected, you shouldn't leave your code open to vulnerabilities.

2.3 Real-World Applications

Ruby is used across various industries, each with its own set of challenges. Let's look at a few examples:

Manufacturing

In manufacturing, Ruby is used to build applications that monitor production lines and manage inventory. For instance, a Ruby application might integrate with sensors on the factory floor to provide real-time data on production metrics, detect anomalies, and trigger alerts if a machine fails.

Case Study:

A manufacturing company used Ruby on Rails to develop a dashboard that aggregates data from multiple sources. Pattern matching was later introduced to simplify the parsing of sensor data streams, making the system more responsive and easier to maintain.

Healthcare

Healthcare applications require stringent security measures and reliable performance. Ruby has been used to develop patient management systems, appointment scheduling apps, and even data processing pipelines for clinical research. Ruby's focus on code readability and maintainability helps ensure that these critical systems are robust and easy to audit.

Case Study:

A healthcare startup built a patient portal using Rails, emphasizing clear API design and secure authentication. By integrating static analysis tools and automated testing, they maintained high code quality and met regulatory compliance.

Logistics

Logistics and supply chain management systems often require complex data processing and real-time tracking. Ruby's flexibility makes it well-suited for building applications that can handle dynamic data, such as shipment tracking, route optimization, and inventory management.

Case Study:

A logistics firm developed an API using Sinatra that provided real-time updates on shipment statuses. The API's design followed RESTful principles and included robust error handling, ensuring that clients received consistent and reliable data.

2.4 Community Engagement and Open Source Contribution

A thriving community is one of Ruby's greatest strengths. Engaging with the community can accelerate your learning, provide valuable networking opportunities, and contribute to the evolution of the language.

How to Contribute to Open Source

- **Start Small:** Begin with minor bug fixes or documentation improvements.

- **Join Projects:** Look for projects on GitHub that welcome contributions.

- **Code Reviews:** Participate in code reviews and discussions to learn best practices.

- **Attend Conferences and Meetups:** Ruby conferences and local user groups are excellent venues to share your knowledge and collaborate with other developers.

Real-World Analogy:
Contributing to open source is like joining a community garden—by helping maintain and improve the space, you not only benefit from the collective effort but also share in the rewards of a thriving, vibrant community.

Continuous Learning

The Ruby community is constantly evolving. Staying current with modern trends means following blogs, participating in forums, and subscribing to newsletters. Engaging in community discussions on platforms like Stack Overflow and Reddit can expose you to diverse perspectives and innovative solutions.

2.5 Key Terminology

- **Pattern Matching:** A feature that allows for deconstructing complex data structures in a concise manner.

- **Ractor:** A concurrency abstraction in Ruby 3 for safe parallel execution.

- **Static Analysis:** The process of analyzing code for potential errors and code quality issues without executing it.

- **DSL (Domain-Specific Language):** A specialized mini-language tailored to a specific problem domain.

- **Open Source:** Software whose source code is freely available for modification and distribution.

- **Community Engagement:** Active participation in forums, meetups, and collaborative projects.

---

3. Tools and Setup

A solid development environment is essential for working with modern Ruby features and engaging with the community. In this section, we detail the tools and steps needed to set up your environment for exploring Ruby 3 enhancements, static analysis, and collaborative development.

3.1 Required Tools

To work effectively with modern Ruby trends, you will need:

- **Ruby Interpreter (Ruby 3+):** To access the latest features like pattern matching and Ractor.

- **Version Manager (RVM or rbenv):** To manage Ruby versions and switch between them easily.

- **Text Editor or IDE:** Visual Studio Code, Sublime Text, or Atom with Ruby plugins.

- **Terminal/Command Prompt:** For running Ruby scripts and interacting with the CLI.

- **Gems:**

  - **RuboCop:** For static code analysis and enforcing style guides.

  - **Brakeman:** For security analysis in Rails applications.

  - **RSpec/Minitest:** For writing automated tests.

- **Git:** For version control and contributing to open source projects.

- **Browser and Postman:** For testing web applications and APIs.

3.2 Installing Ruby 3 with RVM

If you don't have Ruby 3 installed, follow these steps:

1. **Install RVM:**

```bash
```

```bash
\curl -sSL https://get.rvm.io | bash -s stable
```

2. **Install Ruby 3:**

```bash
```

```bash
rvm install ruby --latest
rvm use ruby --default
```

3. **Verify Installation:**

```bash
```

```bash
ruby -v
```

3.3 Configuring Your Text Editor

For Visual Studio Code:

1. **Download VS Code:**

   Visit code.visualstudio.com to download and install.

2. **Install Ruby Extensions:**

   Open the Extensions view (Ctrl+Shift+X) and search for "Ruby" (e.g., Ruby by Peng Lv) and install.

3. **Configure Settings:**

Edit your settings.json file:

```json
json

{

  "editor.tabSize": 2,
  "files.trimTrailingWhitespace": true,
  "ruby.format": "rubocop"
}
```

3.4 Setting Up Static Analysis and Testing Tools

1. **RuboCop:**

Install via gem:

```bash
bash

gem install rubocop
Create a .rubocop.yml file in your project:
yaml

AllCops:
  TargetRubyVersion: 3.0
Layout/LineLength:
  Max: 100
Style/StringLiterals:
  EnforcedStyle: double_quotes
```

2. **Brakeman (for Rails projects):**

```bash
bash
```

```
gem install brakeman
```

3. **RSpec:**

Add to your Gemfile:

```ruby
```

```
group :test do
  gem 'rspec'
end
```

Then run:

```bash
```

```
bundle install
rspec --init
```

3.5 Git and Community Tools

- **Git:**

    Install Git and configure it for version control:

```bash
```

```
git config --global user.name "Your Name"
git config --global user.email
"your.email@example.com"
```

- **Postman:**

    Download and install Postman for API testing.

- **Browser:**

  Ensure you have a modern web browser for testing web applications.

---

4. Hands-on Examples & Projects

This section provides detailed, practical examples that demonstrate modern Ruby features and community best practices. We start with smaller examples that illustrate new language features and best practices, then build a comprehensive project: developing a to-do API with complete testing instructions.

4.1 Example 1: Using Pattern Matching
Exercise: Basic Pattern Matching Example

Create a file named pattern_matching.rb:

```ruby

# pattern_matching.rb
def identify(value)
  case value
  in Integer
    "It's an integer."
  in String
    "It's a string."
  in [Integer, Integer]
    "It's an array of two integers."
```

```ruby
    else
      "Unknown type."
    end
  end
```

```ruby
puts identify(42)            # => "It's an integer."
puts identify("Ruby")        # => "It's a string."
puts identify([1, 2])        # => "It's an array of
two integers."
puts identify([1, "two"])    # => "Unknown type."
```

Explanation:

This example demonstrates how Ruby 3's pattern matching can simplify type checking and deconstruct complex data structures.

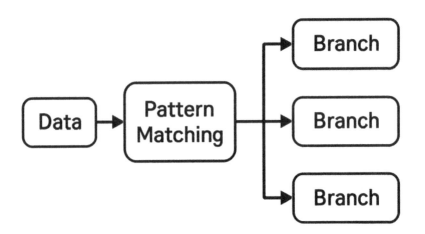

4.2 Example 2: Working with Ractor
Exercise: Parallel Processing with Ractor

Create a file named ractor_example.rb:

```ruby

# ractor_example.rb
ractor = Ractor.new do
  sleep 1
  "Processed in parallel with Ractor"
end

puts "Waiting for Ractor..."
result = ractor.take
puts result  # => "Processed in parallel with Ractor"
```

Explanation:

This simple example demonstrates Ractor's ability to run code concurrently, bypassing the limitations of traditional threads in Ruby.

Conclusion & Next Steps

Recap of Key Points

In this chapter, we explored the fundamentals of web development and RESTful API design using Ruby. We examined popular web frameworks such as Sinatra and Ruby on Rails and discussed the architectural principles of REST, MVC, and CRUD operations. Through a series of practical examples and a comprehensive project—a to-do API with complete testing instructions—you learned how to build scalable, maintainable web applications that adhere to modern best practices.

Reflecting on the Project

The to-do API project was designed to illustrate the full lifecycle of API development, from designing endpoints to writing tests that ensure reliability. By building a project that supports all CRUD operations, you gained valuable insights into HTTP request handling, JSON processing, error handling, and automated testing. This hands-on experience is a solid foundation upon which you can build more complex applications.

Advanced Techniques and Optimization

We also discussed advanced techniques such as caching, database integration, API versioning, and security enhancements. These strategies are essential for building APIs that perform well under real-world conditions and are robust enough to handle future changes without breaking existing functionality.

Troubleshooting and Continued Learning

Troubleshooting is an integral part of development. By adopting a systematic approach—using logging, interactive debugging, and isolated testing—you can quickly identify and resolve issues.

Continuous learning, whether through community engagement or studying open source projects, is key to mastering web development and API design.

Next Steps

To further enhance your skills:

- **Expand Your Projects:** Consider adding user authentication, advanced search features, or integration with external services.

- **Explore Further:** Delve deeper into Rails for full-stack development, or experiment with microservice architectures using Sinatra.

- **Engage with the Community:** Participate in open-source projects, attend Ruby conferences, and join local user groups to stay updated.

- **Invest in Testing:** Build comprehensive test suites and integrate continuous integration tools to automate testing.

Final Thoughts

Web development and RESTful API design are dynamic fields that continue to evolve. By mastering the core concepts and best practices presented in this chapter—from building simple applications with Sinatra to designing robust APIs with clear testing strategies—you're well-prepared to tackle modern software challenges. Embrace the journey of continuous learning and improvement, and let your passion for coding drive you to create applications that are not only functional but also elegant and resilient.

www.ingramcontent.com/pod-product-compliance
Lightning Source LLC
Chambersburg PA
CBHW071237050326
40690CB00011B/2161